Great Bread Machine Recipes

Norman A. Garrett

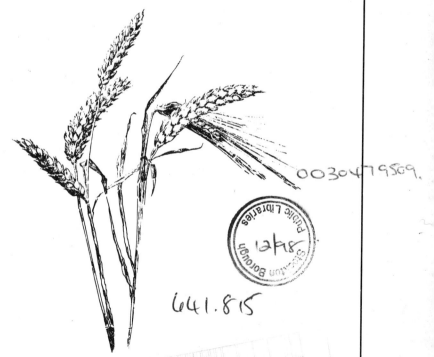

Sterling Publ

Library of Congress Cataloging-in-Publication Data

Garrett, Norman A.
    Great bread machine recipes / Norman A. Garrett.
        p.   cm.
    Includes index.
    ISBN 0-8069-8724-3
    1. Bread.   2. Automatic bread machines.   I. Title.
    TX769.G37   1992
    641.8′15—dc20

92-16781
CIP

10 9 8

Published in 1992 by Sterling Publishing Company, Inc.
387 Park Avenue South, New York, N.Y. 10016
© 1992 by Norman A. Garrett
Distributed in Canada by Sterling Publishing
% Canadian Manda Group, P.O. Box 920, Station U
Toronto, Ontario, Canada M8Z 5P9
Distributed in Great Britain and Europe by Cassell PLC
Villiers House, 41/47 Strand, London WC2N 5JE, England
Distributed in Australia by Capricorn Link Ltd.
P.O. Box 665, Lane Cove, NSW 2066
Manufactured in the United States of America

Sterling ISBN 0-8069-8724-3

Acknowledgments

This book could not have been written without the assistance of several bread tasters. The following people assisted by tasting recipes and giving good, honest feedback: Terry and Carol Lundgren, Heather Hart, Alan and Gina Bagley, and April Barnett.

Other people gave encouragement to the project by contributing recipes, including some old family favorites. In this regard, I appreciate the help of Pat Graves and Carol Lundgren, two of my colleagues at Eastern Illinois University, who were fascinated by the project and the concept of bread machines.

Those who really bore the brunt of this project, however, were the members of my family: my wife, Margie, and my children, Rachel, Ethan, Josh, Aaron, and Emily. As with most family members, they were not afraid to let me know when they thought a recipe needed help, and they were not above making suggestions—some of which were used with great success!

Finally, I appreciate the fact that my mother, Mrs. Betty Cramer, bought me my first bread machine and really got this project going with her encouragement and knowledge of baking and bread ingredients.

NORMAN A. GARRETT

CONTENTS

INTRODUCTION

As soon as I unpacked my new bread machine, I discovered two things: It was very easy to use, and there were no recipes available for it. I searched the bookstores, looked in *Books in Print*, scoured the public libraries, and asked everyone I knew who had a machine, all to no avail. So, I took the basic recipes that came with the machine and began to alter them, experiment with different ingredients, convert old family recipes, and search for any idea that sounded good.

After I overcame my fear of experimenting with my machine, I began to record the good recipes and to make notes on the bad ones for future reference. Once I figured out how the machine worked, I wrote some computer software to assist me in developing recipes. The software helped me experiment with fewer failures, and I began to formulate a set of parameters for bread machine recipes that, when adhered to, usually yielded good results.

The result of this work and experimentation is this book. It contains many different types of recipes using different types of grains, flours, seeds, and other ingredients. Trying different kinds of breads is an exciting and tantalizing activity, particularly for bread lovers. In addition, it gives you total control over what you eat. In these times of heightened health consciousness, knowing what you are eating is a high priority.

These breads contain only natural ingredients, and this allows you to control what you are eating. With a bread machine, you can select recipes that not only appeal to your palate but give you the nutritional boost you are seeking. Diets need not eliminate bread, as long as you can produce wholesome bread with few empty calories. To help you evaluate the recipes, I have calculated the nutritional values for each of the loaves of bread in this book.

There are many bread machines on the market, and not all will bake the same. The machines vary in their motor size, baking capacity, cycle types and lengths, baking options, and appearance. In testing these recipes on different machines, I found considerable variation in the quality of the bread produced by the different machines. Most of the recipes in this book were tested on Hitachi and Welbilt machines. I have tried to adjust the recipes to work in most machines, but where modifications might be necessary, they are indicated in the recipes. Be sure to read all the notes for each recipe.

Feel free to experiment. Experimentation allowed me to develop most of the recipes in this book. You can do the same. Once you become familiar with the basic ingredients of bread, you will be able to make substitutions, convert old (standard) bread recipes, and even produce your own creations.

Consider these recipes as a beginning and make your own notes in the margins of this book. Watch the machine work. Become familiar with its sounds, its cycles, and the texture of the doughs it produces. Familiarity with your machine will lead to the desire to strike out on your own to try new and wonderful tastes in bread. Happy baking!

GETTING TO KNOW YOUR BREAD MAKER

Basic Operation

Although bread machines come in various shapes, sizes, and capacities, they all share common characteristics and principles of operation. They are all designed to make bread making easy, quick, and complete. Other than your placing the proper ingredients in the baking pan, pressing a few buttons, and removing the bread when it is finished (and slicing it, of course), the machine does all the work.

After the ingredients are placed in the pan and you start the machine, the following cycles are completed:

1. The initial mix cycle
2. The first rise
3. The "punch down"
4. The second rise
5. The bake
6. The cool down

The length of each cycle will depend on the make and model of your machine. Some machines skip the second rise and bake after the first rise. Other machines have alternate settings that let you select a double or single rise (often called the "quick bread" cycle). Whatever your machine's configuration, you need to become familiar with the way it works so that you can tap its full potential for making delicious loaves of bread.

Capacities and Limitations

Each machine has a maximum capacity and limitation. Capacities are usually either 1 pound or 1½ pounds. Because overloading the machine can cause motor damage or dough overflows, it is not wise to exceed the rated capacity of your machine.

What about baking a loaf smaller than the rated capacity? On most machines, that will work fine. The recipes in this book are presented in both 1-pound and 1½-pound sizes. If you have a 1-pound machine, limit yourself to baking the 1-pound loaves. If you have a 1½-pound machine, feel free to try both recipe sizes.

Table 1 shows the basic capacities of bread machines currently on the market. You can determine the capacity of your machine from the owner's manual or by checking the white-bread recipe that came with the machine. If the recipe calls for 2 cups of bread flour, you have a 1-pound machine. If it calls for 3 or more cups, you have a 1½-pound (or greater) capacity machine.

Table 1: Bread Machine Capacities

Flour Amount (Basic White-Bread Recipe)	1 Pound	1½ Pound	1½ + Pound
2	X		
2.5	X		
3		X	
3.5			X
3.4			X

Note: Determine the amount of flour called for in the basic white-bread recipe for your machine. This chart will tell you the capacity of your machine based on that amount. If you do not have access to the basic white-bread recipe that came with your machine, assume it to be a 1-pound capacity.

Baking the Dough Yourself

All of these machines let you bake the dough yourself. Simply extract the dough after the first rise is complete. If your machine has a dough setting, it will beep when it is time to remove the dough. You can then punch it down, knead it, and place it in bread pans or on cookie sheets for a final rise and baking.

Adding Ingredients

Some machines have a "mix bread" setting, which will beep when it is time to add raisins, seeds, or other ingredients to the dough. Since not all machines have this capability, I have developed the recipes in this book so that all ingredients can be placed in the pan in the beginning. However, if you have a "mix" cycle, you can use that cycle, particularly in the recipes calling for seeds, nuts, or raisins.

Crusts

The baking times vary on bread machines. Most machines offer you the option of selecting the darkness of your crust. The control for this will usually determine the baking temperature of your bread and will not alter the length of the baking cycle. Setting the control for a darker crust will increase the temperature of the oven. On the other hand, I found that turning the dial on the Welbilt machine to the lightest crust setting actually caused some breads to have uncooked dough in the middle. It will probably take a few loaves for you to determine the optimum setting to accommodate both your machine's capabilities and your personal taste. Once you determine that setting, make a note of it, because you will probably want to bake all of your loaves with that same setting.

Knowing Your Own Machine

You will need to get used to your particular machine. In testing for this book, I found considerable variations between the different machines I used. Become familiar with two parts of the baking process as they apply to your specific machine: the optimum consistency of your dough and the sound of your machine as it goes through the cycles.

Dough Consistency

Dough consistency and each machine's ability to deal with different dough consistencies are important and vary widely. Some machines work best with a runny dough (more liquid content). Others have powerful motors that can easily handle stiffer doughs. Observe your bread as it mixes. Make a mental note of the dough consistency. Then, when the bread is finished, note the texture of the bread. Learn to compare the finished texture to the consistency of the dough. Soon, you will be able to accurately predict the texture of the bread by looking at the dough immediately after mixing. This skill is important if you want to make any recipe modifications.

Machine Sounds

As you use your machine, also note the typical sounds it makes as it progresses though its various cycles. Once you become familiar with the "normal" sounds, you will be aware when the motor is making unusual noises, indicating that the motor is being overworked, which can damage the machine.

Service and Cleaning

Cleaning

If you want consistently good bread from your machine, make sure it remains clean. Take two or three minutes after each loaf has baked to clean the machine. This will yield consistently better loaves and will assure that your machine stays in peak operating condition.

The difficulty of cleaning the machines varies by their design. The Hitachi and similar machines use a bucket with the beater drive mechanism built in. Consequently, cleaning is simply a matter of removing the bread from the bucket, removing the beater, and cleaning the bucket with warm water. On the Welbilt, the beater drive mechanism is not part of the bucket and must be cleaned after each use. This cleaning is more difficult and sometimes results in crumbs in the bottom of the baking chamber.

I have found that a damp kitchen washcloth will pick up most crumbs from the baking chamber. I have tried mini-vacuums, canned air, and other methods such as turning the whole unit upside down and shaking it, but find the simple washcloth the best (and least messy).

All machines have a special, non-stick surface in the bread pan. Take care with this surface. Do not use any abrasive cleaners or scouring pads on the inside of the bread pan, or you will damage the non-stick surface. Try not to pry stuck breads with knives, forks, or other hard objects that may scratch the surface. If you must pry, use a rubber or soft plastic device of some kind (like a rubber spatula). If you take care of your bread pan, it will give you many future loaves of bread.

The machines, such as the Welbilt and DAK, in which the beater mechanism is part of the housing rather than the bread bucket, also have a small plastic washer. Be careful with this washer. Don't lose it, and rinse it off and dry it after each loaf of bread. Without the washer, you will not have a good seal between the bucket and the bottom of the baking chamber, and leakage will occur.

If you have an accident with your bread machine (overflow or other big mess), wait until it cools down and take your time cleaning it. Most baked-on bread can be removed with warm water, and that is the recommended cleanup. I have had my share of disasters, and I have managed to clean all of them up without even using soap. Just warm water and a washcloth have always been all that is needed.

Lost and Damaged Parts

There are generally no user-serviceable components in the bread machine, other than those just mentioned. However, there are parts that are easily lost or damaged, which you can replace yourself. Most prominent on the list is the mixer beater. Since it is a small, removable part, it is easily misplaced. Make sure that you replace the beater in the bucket after each cleaning. That will minimize the potential for losing it.

The plastic washer that fits beneath the bread bucket will wear out over time. If your machine has one of these, it might be a good idea to order a replacement to have on hand, since it is an inexpensive item.

The Bread Pan

The other major removable component is the bread pan itself. Be careful of the non-stick surface. If you damage the surface to the point where bread sticks to it, you have to replace the bread pan. As long as you are able to remove the bread from the pan, don't worry about small scratches.

Major Repairs

If any other problems arise with your machine, then you will probably have to send it in for repair. The control panel, for example, will sometimes cease to function and will need to be replaced. You should obtain an estimate before authorizing any major repairs on your machine, because it is possible that the cost of repairs will exceed the cost of the machine. The likelihood is that your machine will have a long, productive life, and that it will give you many hours of trouble-free bread baking if you will simply keep it clean and ready for the next loaf.

Troubleshooting Guide

There are many variables that can affect your bread. Those listed below are all problems I have experienced while making bread in my own machines. You may encounter some not listed here. Before you write off the bread machine completely or send it out for repairs, think the problem through and make sure that you have accounted for all the possible reasons for the problem. These would include crust settings, proper baking cycles, measuring ingredients properly, using fresh ingredients, checking for power outages during baking (which will recycle your machine), and, finally, curious children pushing buttons.

Dough beater is stuck If your dough beater is difficult to remove after baking a loaf of bread, try using some shortening on the shaft before installing the beater and placing dry ingredients in the pan first. In the machines where the beater is self-contained in the pan, soak the beater in water for a few minutes after removing the bread. In the Welbilt/DAK-type machines, the beater will stay with the loaf of bread and is rarely a problem to remove.

Leakage of the liquid into baking chamber This might be a problem on the DAK/Welbilt machines or others whose pans have a hole in the bottom to accommodate the dough beater. These machines should have dry ingredients placed in the bread pan first. Liquids should be added last. Also, check to make sure that you have the rubber sealing washer in the proper position before locking the pan in place. Then make sure that the pan is securely locked before adding ingredients.

The recipe just doesn't work Make sure that you have added the proper quantities. It is easy to become distracted while setting up a recipe and miscount your ingredients. Also, check that you chose the correct settings when baking the bread. Finally, be sure that your ingredients are fresh and that the proper type of ingredient has been used.

The size of the loaf seems to vary, even though the weight is the same The size of your loaf will vary according to the ingredients. While the weight of two loaves of bread may be the same, their size and appearance may vary greatly. This is due to the different ingredients used. In general, breads using gluten-rich bread flour will rise more than breads using flours with less gluten content. Rye breads, for example, will be small and will have a dense texture with a dark crust. The loaf sizes of the recipes in this book refer to weight, not to finished size.

Spoiled ingredients You must be cautious with fresh eggs and fresh milk. Do not use either of these ingredients in a "delay bake" cycle (available on some machines), where you set the timer to start the bread at a later time. Milk would be all right if the delay were not more than an hour or two, but I would not recommend that eggs be used in any recipe that will not be started immediately. If you want to use a recipe calling for eggs on a delay bake, consider using powdered eggs instead of fresh eggs. If you want to use milk in a delayed recipe, use dry milk and add the proper amount of water to compensate.

Dough rises too high, then collapses Your dough probably rose too long. Since the timer cycles are not programmable on most machines, you may consider reducing the yeast by ½ teaspoon to get less rising. Check to make sure that the machine was not recycled during the process. Recycling can occur after brief power outages. It may also occur when children (or curious adults) press machine buttons. If a power outage occurs and you are aware of it, you can remove the dough from the machine and finish the process by hand, baking the bread in the oven.

The bread has a strong yeast flavor It is possible that too much yeast was added. Cut the yeast down by ½ teaspoon and try again.

The loaf does not rise This can be a complex problem with many possible causes. Any of the following will inhibit rising:

- Using flour with low-gluten content (pure rye flour, wheat flour, etc.).
- Too much salt in the recipe. Salt is a yeast inhibitor.
- Too little sugar in the recipe. Sugar feeds yeast and promotes rising.
- Old yeast. Yeast expires. Check your yeast supply and make sure you are using fresh yeast. Old yeast will not activate and rise properly.
- Dead yeast. This may be caused by adding hot ingredients. For example, if your recipe calls for some ingredients to be boiled before being added to the mix, do not add them until they have had time to cool. Adding ingredients that are too hot will kill your yeast.

The bread has an uneven top This usually indicates too little liquid in the recipe. However, on some breads, such as rye breads, where less rising takes place, this may be a normal occurrence.

The bread has a collapsed top This is usually caused by too much liquid in the recipe. Cut the liquid back by 2 tablespoons and try again. Be careful not to make your bread dough too stiff, because some machines have underpowered motors that will not be able to handle stiffer dough, particularly in the 1½-pound recipes. Also be aware that some recipes use ingredients that are going to add liquid to the dough during the baking cycle, and a collapsed top might be normal. I found that breads using fresh cheeses generally fall into this category.

The bread has a rancid taste Check your whole-grain ingredients. Whole-grain flours, wheat germ, and similar ingredients should be kept in the refrigerator or freezer. They spoil rapidly when left at room temperature. White flours are not subject to the same type of spoilage and can be left in the cupboard.

There are white spots on the side of the loaf This is flour that has stuck to the side of the pan during the mixing process and has not mixed into the dough. When the bread rises and bakes, this flour sticks to the outside of the loaf. While not a taste problem, it can present a cosmetic problem. The solution is to look into the baking pan after the mixing has taken place. If there is flour stuck to the sides of the pan, take a rubber spatula, remove it from the sides, and mix it in with the dough.

The crust is soggy You left the bread in the pan too long after the baking cycle completed. Some machines have cooling cycles that will cool the bread and remove the moisture. Soggy crust is not as great a problem on these machines, but it is still a good idea to remove the bread and place it on a cooling rack as soon as the final beep is heard.

The dough did not seem to be properly mixed This happened to me when I forgot to replace the dough beater after cleanup from the previous loaf. Now I watch the initial mix for a minute or so when I first turn the machine on. I can see the mixing taking place. If the motor is running, but no mixing is happening, check the dough beater. If it has been left out, stop the machine, replace the beater, and start the cycle over.

The loaves are not consistent in size and texture If you bake the same recipe and get different results, blame the weather. Weather is actually a large factor in baking, as temperature and humidity have substantial control over the amount of dough rising that will take place.

The dough beater is lost If you have the type of machine where the beater stays in the loaf when the bread is removed from the baking pan, check the last loaf of bread. I had a loaf of bread to give to a friend for testing, only to realize that I was about to give away the dough beater, too! Get in the habit of cleaning your pan right away and putting everything back in the machine. Then your beater will always be where you want it: in the pan ready to bake.

CONVERTING EXISTING RECIPES

Naturally, after you have had time to experiment with your bread machine, you are going to want to try great-grandma's recipe. However, you will notice that her recipe was not designed to work in a bread machine. But, fortunately, most yeast-bread recipes can be converted to work in bread machines.

Converting a recipe to work in your machine is not difficult, but it is computationally intensive work. Have a calculator handy if you want to attempt a conversion. You'll also want a sheet or two of paper to write down the totals for the new, converted recipe.

This chapter will take you through the steps for converting a "regular" recipe to one you can try in your machine. It may take one or two trials to perfect the recipe, but the chances are good that you can successfully make the conversion. Before converting a recipe, make sure that it is a yeast-bread recipe. Bread machines are not designed to handle batter breads.

The four basic steps in making the conversion are:

1. Cut the recipe down so that it will make one loaf. Many recipes are designed to make two loaves. You will need to cut these in half, because you will need a single-loaf recipe.
2. Determine the parameters of your particular bread machine.
3. Determine the liquidity ratio of the recipe. This ratio is the "stiffness" of the dough. This is important because your machine has a rather narrow range of doughs it can handle.
4. Determine the overall bulk of the recipe. You do not want a recipe that is too large for your machine.

Let's look at each of these steps in turn, with particular attention to the details involved in each step. Once you have accomplished a few conversions, you won't need to refer to this book, because the steps are not really so complex as they might seem at first.

Step One: Reduce the Recipe Size

Most recipes will tell you how many loaves they make. Some will even tell you the approximate size of each loaf. Cut the recipe so that it will make one loaf and write down the new recipe.

If the recipe doesn't say how many loaves it makes, you can make a rough judgment by looking at the amount of flour required. A 1-pound loaf of bread will require about 2 cups of flour. Thus, if your recipe calls for 6 cups of all-purpose flour, you can probably figure that it will make three 1-pound loaves or two 1½-pound loaves.

Step Two: Determine the Parameters of Your Machine

Since each machine varies in its capacity and motor power, you must determine the acceptable ranges for your machine in two categories: liquidity ratio and bulk. Table 2 shows the acceptable liquidity-ratio ranges. To find your machine's range, look at the basic white-bread

Table 2: Bread Machine Liquidity Ratios

Ounces Liquid 1/8 c = 1 oz	Cups of Flour			
	2	2½	3	3½
5	2.9–3.5	3.6–4.4	4.3–5.3	5.0–6.2
6	2.4–3.0	3.0–3.6	3.6–4.4	4.2–5.2
7	2.1–2.5	2.6–3.2	3.1–3.7	3.6–4.4
8	1.8–2.2	2.3–2.8	2.7–3.3	3.2–3.9
9	1.6–2.0	2.0–2.4	2.4–3.0	2.8–3.4
10	1.4–1.8	1.8–2.2	2.2–2.6	2.5–3.1
11	1.4–1.7	1.6–2.0	2.0–2.4	2.3–2.8

Notes:
1. Shaded boxes indicate the most common bread machine ratio ranges.
2. Ratio is computed by dividing dry ingredients by liquid.
3. Higher ratios indicate stiffer dough; lower ratios indicate more liquid dough.

recipe that came with the machine. Determine the number of cups of flour called for. Follow that column until you find the row that shows the number of ounces of liquid (water or milk) called for in the recipe. In that box you will find the ratio range for your machine. Highlight or write down the ratio range. (On page 124 in the Appendix, you can note this and other information about your bread machine.)

Bulk is determined by the number of cups of flour called for in the basic white-bread recipe for your machine. If the recipe calls for 2–2½ cups of flour, you have a 1-pound machine. If the recipe calls for 3–4 cups of flour, you have a 1½-pound (or greater) machine.

Once you know the parameters of your machine, you can skip this step and move right from Step One to Step Three.

Step Three: Determine the Liquidity Ratio of the Recipe

Now, you must determine the liquidity ratio (dough stiffness) of the recipe you are trying to convert. Table 3 is a handy chart that you can duplicate and use each time you convert a recipe. To use the chart, simply fill in the ingredients and the amount called for in the original recipe. Write the amount in decimals (so that your calculator can add them later) in the appropriate column. For example, if the recipe calls for 2½ cups of flour, enter 2.5 in the DRY Cup column. You will have to determine whether the ingredient is dry or wet. In general, use the form that the ingredient is in when you add it. An exception to this would be an ingredient that is going to melt when heat is applied. Typical ingredients in this category would include butter, margarine, fresh cheese, and shortening.

Some ingredients should not be computed. Do not include the following ingredients in the calculation:

1. Yeast
2. Raisins or nuts added at the mix cycle
3. Seeds added at the mix cycle

You should count raisins, nuts, and seeds added initially as dry ingredients. The general rule is that if the ingredient will add to the stiffness of the dough, count it as a dry ingredient.

After you have entered all the ingredients, total each column and place the sum in the subtotal box. Then multiply each subtotal by the multiplier specified and place the result in the total box. Add the totals for dry together for a grand total and do the same for wet ingredients. Finally, divide the dry grand total by the wet grand total to compute the ratio for this recipe.

For best results, the ratio should fall within the liquidity-ratio-range designation for your machine (see Step Two). If it only misses by a few points, it will probably be satisfactory. If the ratio for the recipe is below the range, your dough might be too wet. Try a slight reduction in liquid ingredients or an increase in dry ingredients and recalculate. If the ratio is above the range, it is too dry. Either reduce the dry ingredients slightly or add liquid.

Chances are, you will still need to experiment to get the recipe just right, but this calculation will give you a good start and place you well beyond the "trial and error" stage.

Table 3: Dough Liquidity Calculation Worksheet

Ingredient	DRY			WET			
	tsp	tbs	cup	tsp	tbs	cup	oz
Subtotal							
Multiplier		3	48		3	48	6
TOTAL							
GRAND TOTAL							
LIQUIDITY RATIO							

Instructions:
1. Use decimals for fractions (.5 teaspoon, etc.).
2. Use a calculator to subtotal each column.
3. Multiply the subtotal by the multiplier to obtain the total.
4. Add the dry totals and wet totals separately to obtain the grand total.
5. Divide the dry grand total by the wet grand total to get the liquidity ratio.

Step Four: Determine the Overall Bulk

You certainly do not want to overflow your machine with your test recipe, so make sure that the bulk does not exceed the capacity of your machine. If you have a 1-pound machine, your recipe should not call for more than 2½ cups of flour. A 1½-pound machine is limited to about 3½ cups of flour. If you need to fine-tune the recipe, be sure you make equal adjustments to both the wet and dry ingredients to maintain the liquidity ratio of the recipe.

Improving and Tailoring Your Recipes

After your initial attempt at your newly converted recipe, you may want to adjust the recipe to increase or decrease the bulk, to reduce or increase the rise, or to alter the texture or taste. Experiment with the recipe until you have perfected it. Part of the enjoyment of a bread machine is being able to try new and exciting recipes and to be creative. Although the conversion process, as presented here, may seem somewhat better suited to a mathematician than an artist, science and art go hand in hand in bread baking. Once you get to know your machine and your ingredients, you will feel comfortable making substitutions or even trying brand-new creations from scratch.

RECIPE POINTERS

Recipe Sizes

Two sizes are given for each of the recipes in this book. Smaller sizes are possible, but I don't recommend them. In experimenting, I found that the machines tended to overbake ¾-pound loaves and that they typically were too dry. Consequently, I decided to present only the two sizes that can be accommodated by virtually all bread machines.

Recipe sizes refer to finished weight, not dimensions. The finished dimensions of the bread will depend to a great extent on baking conditions, amounts of yeast used, and types of ingredients. A 1-pound loaf of white bread, for example, might be larger than a 1½-pound loaf of rye bread, which tends to be more densely textured.

Modifications for Specific Machines

I have tried to include recipes that will work in any machine. With the 1-pound recipes, I found virtually no difference when testing the recipes in different machines. With the 1½-pound loaves, however, I noted that some machines will not tolerate a stiff dough as well as others. On those recipes, I have noted that you might consider adding 1 or 2 tablespoons more liquid in certain machines. This addition will lower the liquidity ratio slightly, making the dough less stiff. Some motors appear to labor under the load of 1½ pounds of stiff dough. If your machine seems to be having trouble kneading dough, add a little liquid to the recipe. As mentioned previously, you will come to recognize the "normal" sounds of your machine, and you will be able to identify those situations when slight recipe modifications are needed.

The other major difference between machines is in their rise cycles and the amount of yeast called for. I have tried to optimize the amount of yeast in the recipes to be suitable to all machines. When more yeast is needed for a certain machine, the notes for the recipe will indicate it. Be sure to read the notes for each recipe before trying it. There may be modifications for your particular machine.

A few machines, such as the Hitachi, have "Quick Bread" cycles that allow you to bake a loaf quickly (single rise, rather than the usual double rise). When using this cycle on your machine, double the amount of yeast that is normally called for or consult your owner's manual for the proper yeast adjustment.

Ingredients

There is a wide variety of ingredients called for in these recipes. Many are available at your local supermarket, but some must be purchased at health food stores. Some mail order sources are available if you do not have a health food store nearby. The following is a summary of important information about some of the main ingredients used in the recipes in this book.

White Flours

There are two main types of white flours: all-purpose flour and bread flour. Both varieties are available in most grocery stores. Bread flour is higher in gluten content than all-purpose flour, and it will rise more. Most of the recipes in this book call for bread flour; however, there are a few that specifically call for all-purpose flour. You should use the type called for by the recipe. Substituting all-purpose flour for bread flour is permissible, but it will slightly change the texture of the bread and cause it to rise less.

Whole Grains

Whole-wheat flour   This flour is ground from the complete wheat berry and contains the wheat germ and the wheat bran. It is coarser and heavier than white flour, and it does not rise as much. I purchase fresh wheat in bulk and grind it myself for the best-tasting bread, but this is beyond the capability of most people. Grocery stores carry whole-wheat flour, usually right alongside the white flour.

Bran   Bran is the outer covering of the kernel of wheat or oat. It is rich in fibre and is called for in small quantities in some recipes. Recently, much has been said about the benefits of oat bran. Both oat and wheat bran are available at most grocery stores.

Wheat germ   This part of the wheat grain is readily available in grocery stores. Like bran, it is used sparingly in recipes. Wheat germ should be kept in the refrigerator after the container is opened.

Rye flour   Rye is very low in gluten content, and it will not rise when used by itself. You will note that most of the recipes in this book call for a mixture of rye and another flour with a higher gluten content that will let the bread rise. The recipe for Bohemian Rye Bread, however, uses pure rye flour to which gluten is added, creating a very dense loaf.

Barley flour   Barley flour lends a sweet taste and smooth texture to bread. Most recipes call for it in combination with white or wheat flour. You will probably have to go to a health food store to find barley flour.

Cracked wheat   As its name implies, this is part of the wheat berry. It is very hard and usually requires some soaking before use. Cracked wheat is widely available at health food stores and can often also be found in grocery stores.

Seven-grain cereal This cereal has an appearance similar to cracked wheat. It consists of seven grains, including wheat, barley, corn, and oats. It is available at health food stores.

Oats Use rolled oats (oatmeal) for your oat recipes. Just use the type available at the grocery store. When measuring rolled oats, pack them down into the measuring cup to get a full measure.

Quinoa This flour is imported from South America. It was a staple grain of the Incas in ancient times. Quinoa has one of the highest protein contents of any grain. It gives bread a somewhat nutty flavor.

Buckwheat This is a strong-tasting flour, which has attracted a loyal band of aficionados. Buckwheat is usually used in small quantities, but if you like its strong flavor, there is an excellent buckwheat-bread recipe in the "whole grains" section of this book.

Liquids

Water is called for in most recipes. It should be used warm (between 100 and 110 degrees). I have found that hot tap water works fine. Don't heat the water any further, because water that is too hot can kill the yeast.

Milk When milk is called for in a recipe, I use 1 percent or skim milk. In fact, the nutritional counts in the recipes in this book are calculated using values for 1 percent milk. If you do not have milk on hand, try using dry milk and adding the requisite amount of water to the recipe. Milk should usually be warmed to 100–110 degrees. The microwave works well for this at 45 seconds on HIGH. Be careful not to add overheated milk to the mix, or you will kill the yeast.

Buttermilk You can use buttermilk in its fresh form, or you can purchase buttermilk powder and mix it as needed. I do the latter. I don't particularly like to drink buttermilk, and recipes usually only call for small amounts. In most recipes, it is safe to substitute low-fat or skim milk for buttermilk. You may sacrifice some flavor, but your bread will have a lower fat content.

Eggs All the recipes in this book have been formulated to call for whole eggs rather than portions of eggs or egg whites. However, if you are concerned about the cholesterol in eggs, you may use any commercially available egg substitute. Use ¼ cup (4 tablespoons) of egg substitute to replace each whole egg. For powdered eggs, use ¼ cup of mixed eggs instead of one whole egg.

Butter Many of the recipes in this book call for butter. You may substitute margarine or vegetable oil in the same quantities. Butter, however, will provide the most flavor. I keep my butter in the freezer, because spoilage is a big problem with real butter. When I need butter, I remove it from the freezer, cut the required quantity from the cube, and return the butter to the freezer. It only takes a few minutes for the cut portion to reach room temperature.

Olive oil I have used olive oil exclusively in these recipes. I think olive oil tastes best. Additionally, olive oil has no cholesterol. However, if you prefer another type of cooking oil, such as canola, corn oil, or any other vegetable oil, you may freely substitute. If you use olive oil, use a good grade of extra-virgin olive oil.

Other Ingredients

Salt   Salt, a yeast inhibitor, is necessary in most recipes. If you are on a salt-restricted diet, you can eliminate the salt from the recipes. You should know, however, that if you do so, the characteristics of the bread will change. It will rise differently, and it may rise too much and then collapse. The resulting texture may also be different. Keep in mind that other ingredients often have salt content. If you are on a salt-restricted diet, check the nutritional values for each recipe to see if there are "hidden salts" in the recipe. Butter, for example, is one of the ingredients that has a sodium content. Avoid using salt substitutes as alternatives. They are chemically based and do not have the yeast-inhibiting properties of real salt. Not only will they do no good, but they may cause other chemical reactions that will change the properties of your bread.

Yeast   The recipes in this book call for yeast in teaspoons. I use Red Star active dry yeast, and I buy it in bulk. If kept in the refrigerator, it will last a long time. In fact, with my bread machine running, a supply of yeast doesn't last long at all. If you use cake yeast, you will need to make the conversion from teaspoons. If you purchase yeast in packets at the grocery store, one packet contains one scant tablespoon, or about 2½ teaspoons of yeast. Do not use rapid-rise yeast in these recipes.

Because there are differences in cycle lengths and the yeast-dispensing mechanisms available on a few machines, not all bread machines use the same amount of yeast in the large recipes. If a recipe does not rise enough, try adding an extra ½ teaspoon of yeast.

Yeast feeds on sugars and is inhibited by salts. It likes a warm environment, but too much heat will kill it. Most traditional bread recipes will require you to "proof" your yeast before using it. Proofing involves mixing the yeast with sugar and warm (105–110-degree) water to allow it to become active before adding it to the recipe. Proofing is not necessary with bread machines, but it is a good technique to use if you want to make sure your yeast is active (not too old). Yeast can be placed directly into the bread pan. When it touches liquid, it will begin activating.

Sugars and sweeteners   These are necessary in all bread recipes because they provide food for the yeast. Recipes in this book call for sugar (white, granulated, or brown), honey, syrup, or molasses. Molasses comes in various types, but I use blackstrap when baking. I have tried others, and I haven't noticed any appreciable difference in the outcome, so use whatever molasses you happen to have on hand if a recipe calls for it. By the way, if the recipe calls for olive oil and honey or molasses, measure the olive oil first and don't rinse the spoon off. The honey or molasses will slide right out of the spoon into your pan!

Gluten   Gluten is necessary for rising to occur. White flours contain plenty of gluten, but some whole-grain flours do not. I have found that some gluten flour added to the mix when using a low-gluten flour will make for better rising and texture. Gluten flour can be purchased at any good health food store. A few recipes call for gluten flour, but most make it optional. Some people are allergic to gluten. Those individuals should stick to low-gluten flours, including rye and quinoa.

Dough enhancer This product is difficult to find. Even health food stores may not carry it. You can find it at baking specialty stores or obtain it through mail order. Dough enhancer is a powder produced from tofu (soybean) that makes the dough smoother. Commercial bakers often use dough enhancer to obtain the smooth-textured bread you buy at the store. If you want to try its effects, it is listed as an optional ingredient in some of the recipes.

Spices, nuts, and seeds These ingredients are called for in a wide variety of recipes. I have found most of the spices, seeds, and nuts called for in these recipes at the grocery store. If you cannot find them, you might try your health food store, which will usually stock some of the lesser-known spices. Feel free to experiment with spices, adding more of spices you like and deleting those you do not. Often it is the blend of spices that makes the flavor, rather than any single spice, especially in those recipes calling for two or three different spices.

You will find as you bake more breads, that your spice cabinet enlarges. Eventually, you will have a stock of almost any spice called for in a recipe. Preserving spices and seeds is not a problem, but preserving fresh nuts is. A few recipes call for fresh chopped nuts. Use any type of nuts you enjoy, but keep in mind that nuts will go rancid if not used in a short period. Keep your supply of fresh nuts rotated.

Sourdough starter In the section on sourdough recipes, there is a recipe for a sourdough starter. You can use this recipe, locate another (any good bread-recipe book will have one), or simply get starter from your local bakery or from a friend. Once you have starter going, you can keep it replenished and never run short. Starter is used in sourdough recipes and can be added as you would any other ingredient.

The Order of Ingredients

There are two ways to place ingredients in the baking pan: dry ingredients first or wet ingredients first. Most machines call for dry ingredients first, so that order is used in this book. Actually, dry first will work in all machines, unless you want to use a timed-bake function. In that case, you will not want to activate the yeast until the baking process starts, so wet ingredients will have to go first and yeast last. The machines that recommend dry ingredients first call for yeast as the first ingredient, followed by the other dry ingredients and, finally, the liquids. That is the order followed in these recipes. If your machine calls for wet ingredients first or if you are trying to use a timed-bake feature, add the ingredients to the pan in reverse order from that listed (start at the bottom of the list and work your way to the top).

Preparation of Ingredients

Most bread recipes call for all ingredients to be at room temperature, except for liquids, which are sometimes called for at 105–110 degrees. I have experimented with this and have not had real problems adding refrigerated ingredients. Rather than worry too much about it, just try setting all of your ingredients out first and then add them. Once you get to the refrigerated ingredients, they have usually approached room temperature anyway.

When warm water is called for, it should be in the 105–110 degree range. I used to use a thermometer to make sure that the water was the correct temperature; however, I gave up on that when I found that hot tap water usually falls within this range. Because hot tap water varies, make sure that yours is not too hot. Too hot presents a much bigger problem than too cold.

Milk can either be measured and then left to reach room temperature, or you can use the microwave to warm it up. Just be sure that if you use the microwave, you don't overheat it, which is easy to do. If you overheat it, let it sit until it cools down to below 110 degrees before adding it to the bread pan.

Making Substitutions and Modifications

I would recommend that you try the recipes as-is the first time. Then, if you want to make substitutions or modifications, experiment all you want. I have found that the best way to experiment is to alter one item at a time. If you alter too many things at once and the recipe fails, you will not be able to determine the cause of the failure. However, if you only changed one ingredient, you will know that the alteration was the only variable that could have caused the failure.

You can freely make the substitutions mentioned in the ingredients section, including margarine for butter, low-fat or skim milk for buttermilk, egg substitutes for whole eggs, and all-purpose flour for bread flour. Keep in mind, however, that these substitutions will alter the original recipe somewhat and results will be different.

Avoid the use of chemically based substitutes such as sugar and salt substitutes. These chemically based products may taste the same in coffee or soft drinks, but they break down differently from sodium or sugar in baking environments, and they will not work properly with yeast breads. It is better simply to eliminate salt, for example, than to use a salt substitute. Yeast feeds fine on sugar, but it doesn't have much of a taste for NutraSweet.

Once you have gained a feel for a recipe and for your machine, feel free to experiment. Most of the recipes in this book were developed that way, and you can have a lot of fun trying new and wonderful ideas. It is best to begin with established recipes and make successive alterations until you arrive at the perfect bread. Be sure and keep a log of your changes and the results. That way, you can learn as you go and won't repeat mistakes. It also helps to have a basic understanding of the principles of baking with yeast and of the characteristics of the ingredients you are using.

Slicing Your Bread

When you get that loaf out of the machine, it smells wonderful. In fact, it has probably permeated the whole house with the unmistakable odor of baking bread! You may want to dig in and eat the whole loaf right on the spot. Of course, you can do that. There is nothing better than fresh hot bread. However, if your aim is to slice the bread and keep it for a few days or to use it for tomorrow's breakfast or lunch, then you will need to slice it carefully.

Bread is best sliced after it has had a chance to cool completely. It then regains some of its stiffness and is much easier too handle. Slicing hot bread is a bit like trying to slice jello. As you cut, the bread gives, and it is difficult to get a good straight slice.

For best results, remove your bread from the machine as soon as the "all done" alarm sounds. Place it on a cooling rack and let it cool completely (probably an hour or so). While many machines now include cooling cycles, they cannot completely cool the bread because it is still in the pan where moisture and heat are trapped.

To slice the bread, use a serrated knife, designed especially for slicing bread. Use a sawing motion and let the knife do the work. Putting too much downward pressure on the bread will smash it down and give you uneven slices.

I inherited a meat slicer and don't use it for meat at all. But I have found it to be a wonderful bread slicer. I just set the thickness and the serrated blade cuts right through my cool loaf. If you have a slicer, and your loaf is too big for it (the Welbilt loaves are too big for mine), cut the loaf in half lengthwise, making two half-circles. Then, slice each half-loaf with your slicer.

Nutritional Values

I am convinced that much of the consumer motivation behind the boom in bread machine sales is due to a desire to eat healthier foods. Whole-grain breads are wonderful sources of nutrients, have no chemical preservatives, and taste great.

Each recipe in this book is followed by the nutritional values. I have purposely left the nutritional values at the loaf level, rather than trying to determine the value of a single slice of bread. Obviously, everyone will slice bread differently. If you want to know the nutritional values for a slice of your bread, estimate what percentage of the total loaf the slice is and multiply that number by the nutritional values shown for the size you baked. For example, if a 1½-pound loaf is cut into 10 slices, multiply the nutritional values by .1 to obtain the values for one slice.

The nutritional values are estimates only, and they should not be construed as anything else. They were derived by using the *Encyclopedia of Food Values*, by Corinne T. Netzer (Dell, 1992). Each of the ingredients in the recipes was calculated and totalled for each size of loaf. Here is an explanation of the values used:

Calories are total calories for the loaf.

Protein is measured in grams. Breads are not high in protein content, but when taken with other foods that are high in protein (for example, meats or legumes, such as beans), a healthy combination is made.

Carbohydrates are also measured in grams. Carbohydrates, especially from whole-grain sources, provide a good ratio of nutrients to calories (the opposite of "empty calories") and should constitute 45–48 percent of your daily intake of calories.

Fat is listed as total fat and saturated fat. You should try to reduce the amount of fats in your diet. Saturated fats should be avoided as much as possible. Government recommendations are that you limit your total calories from fat to 30 percent of your daily intake of calories. Saturated-fat calories should be limited to only 10 percent. In addition to giving you the amount of total fat and saturated fat in grams, I have computed the percentage of calories from fat for each recipe. You will note that these breads are very healthful from the standpoint of percentage of calories from fats.

Cholesterol content is measured in milligrams. Cholesterol is only found in animal fats and certain vegetable fats (especially palm oil and coconut oil). Your total dietary cholesterol intake should be limited to 300 milligrams per day.

Sodium, measured in milligrams, can be found in the salt added to the recipe and in the sodium content of some other recipe ingredients. If you are on a low-sodium diet, you can reduce the salt content of the loaf, but remember the limitations discussed previously.

Fibre is a concern to health-conscious people. The fibre content of each recipe is measured in grams. Because fibre takes several forms, the figure given is a total figure that includes both dietary and crude fibre. Most nutritionists recommend at least 25 grams of fibre per day in your diet.

Recipe Notes

Some recipes contain notes regarding variations to be used with certain machines. These notes refer to *classes* of machines. If the note mentions DAK/Welbilt, it is referring to those particular machines or any other machine calling for 1¼ cups of liquid, 3 cups of flour, and 1 package of yeast in its basic 1½-pound white-bread recipe. References to Panasonic/National include any machine calling for 1¼ cups of liquid, 3 cups of flour, and 3 teaspoons of yeast in its basic 1½-pound white-bread recipe. These variations usually only apply to the 1½-pound recipes, although occasionally I have made an alteration for a 1-pound recipe.

Your strategy for testing recipes should be to try the 1-pound loaf first, even if you have a 1½-pound-capacity machine. This plan offers three advantages:

1. You can make sure you like the taste and texture of the bread by using a lesser quantity of ingredients for the first test.
2. You can make sure the bread works well in your machine with fewer ingredients at risk.
3. You can make sure that your particular baking conditions will not produce an oversize loaf, with little risk of a mess if they do.

Once you have tested a bread, make alterations to suit your taste, baking conditions, and machine. For example, you can increase or reduce yeast amounts, change the liquidity, try substitute seeds or nuts, or make other ingredient substitutions. I would highly recommend, however, that you try the recipe once before making your own modifications, so that you will have a basis upon which to make your changes and a point of reference. Then, be creative.

A Final Disclaimer

The nutrient values shown with the recipes in this book are approximations only and are shown strictly for comparison. Because nutrient values will vary according to the product brand, quantity, and type of ingredient used, individuals needing specific nutrient values should compute the values themselves. Neither the author nor the publisher represents these values to reflect the exact nutritional content of these recipes.

Results of these recipes will vary according to climatic conditions, proper use of ingredients, make and model of machine used, and freshness of ingredients. All recipes in this book have been thoroughly tested but not on all available machines. The author and publisher make no guarantee as to the results of an individual recipe baked on a particular machine in a specific situation, since the possible combinations of variables are almost endless.

WHITE
BREADS

These breads are light white breads. While there is some variation in taste and texture throughout, they are all high risers and will make excellent sandwich or dinner breads. Since the volume of these breads can be great, it is recommended that you try the 1-pound sizes first.

Basic White Bread

This is the best basic white-bread recipe I have found for the bread machine. It is consistently good when baked in different machines and goes with about any meal. It also makes excellent toast.

1½-pound	1-pound
1 teaspoon active dry yeast	½ teaspoon active dry yeast
3 tablespoons sugar	2 tablespoons sugar
3 cups bread flour	2 cups bread flour
1½ teaspoons salt	1 teaspoon salt
1½ tablespoons butter	1 tablespoon butter
4½ ounces warm milk	3 ounces warm milk
4½ ounces warm water	3 ounces warm water

Note: For Panasonic/National machines, use 2 teaspoons of yeast for the 1½-pound loaf.

Nutritional Analysis

	1½-pound	1-pound	
Total calories	1837	1234	calories
Total protein	55	36	grams
Total carbohydrates	341	227	grams
Total fat	26	17	grams
Total saturated fat	12	8	grams
Total cholesterol	52	35	milligrams
Total sodium	3276	2184	milligrams
Total fibre	6	4	grams
Calories from fat	13	13	percent

Challah Bread (Jewish Egg Bread)

A festive white bread, challah is rich with eggs, butter, and honey. You will find it much richer than basic white bread.

1½-pound	1-pound
2½ teaspoons active dry yeast	1½ teaspoons active dry yeast
1½ teaspoons poppy seeds	1 teaspoon poppy seeds
3 cups bread flour	2 cups bread flour
1½ teaspoons salt	1 teaspoon salt
3 tablespoons honey	2 tablespoons honey
3 tablespoons butter	2 tablespoons butter
3 eggs	2 eggs
6 ounces warm water	4 ounces warm water

Note: For Panasonic/National machines, use 3½ teaspoons of yeast for the 1½-pound loaf.

Nutritional Analysis

	1½-pound	1-pound	
Total calories	2230	1486	calories
Total protein	72	48	grams
Total carbohydrates	351	234	grams
Total fat	58	39	grams
Total saturated fat	27	18	grams
Total cholesterol	732	488	milligrams
Total sodium	3401	2267	milligrams
Total fibre	7	5	grams
Calories from fat	24	24	percent

Zuñi Bread

This Southwest Indian bread combines the high-rising texture of white bread with the crunchiness of corn bread. It is excellent with a good, hot Southwestern chili. Note that all-purpose flour is used instead of bread flour in this recipe.

1½-pound	*1-pound*
1½ teaspoons active dry yeast	1 teaspoon active dry yeast
2½ cups all-purpose flour	1¾ cups all-purpose flour
¾ cup yellow cornmeal	½ cup yellow cornmeal
1 teaspoon salt	½ teaspoon salt
1½ tablespoons molasses	1 tablespoon molasses
1½ tablespoons olive oil	1 tablespoon olive oil
1 cup warm water	5½ ounces warm water

Notes
1. For Panasonic/National machines, use 2½ teaspoons of yeast for the 1½-pound loaf.
2. For DAK/Welbilt machines, use 1 extra tablespoon of warm water in the 1½-pound recipe only.

Nutritional Analysis

	1½-pound	*1-pound*	
Total calories	1848	1273	calories
Total protein	50	35	grams
Total carbohydrates	341	236	grams
Total fat	29	20	grams
Total saturated fat	4	3	grams
Total cholesterol	0	0	milligrams
Total sodium	2194	1107	milligrams
Total fibre	16	11	grams
Calories from fat	14	14	percent

Light Wheat Bread

Light wheat is the kind of bread that you buy at the grocery store when you purchase wheat sandwich bread. A light, textured white bread with a hint of wheat taste and a light-brown color, it makes great sandwich bread.

1½-pound	*1-pound*
1 teaspoon active dry yeast	¾ teaspoon active dry yeast
3 tablespoons sugar	2 tablespoons sugar
1½ tablespoons dry milk	1 tablespoon dry milk
2½ cups bread flour	1½ cups bread flour
1½ teaspoons salt	1 teaspoon salt
½ cup whole-wheat flour	5 tablespoons whole-wheat flour
1½ tablespoons butter	1 tablespoon butter
9 ounces warm water	5½ ounces warm water

Note: For Panasonic/National machines, use 2 teaspoons of yeast for the 1½-pound loaf and 1 teaspoon for the 1-pound loaf.

Nutritional Analysis

	1½-pound	*1-pound*	
Total calories	1767	1087	calories
Total protein	53	33	grams
Total carbohydrates	333	204	grams
Total fat	24	16	grams
Total saturated fat	12	8	grams
Total cholesterol	48	32	milligrams
Total sodium	3253	2168	milligrams
Total fibre	13	8	grams
Calories from fat	12	13	percent

Light Rye Bread

This bread has just a hint of rye flavor and a light-brown color. It has the texture of white bread and is excellent sandwich bread, particularly for ham-and-cheese sandwiches.

1½-pound	1-pound
1 teaspoon active dry yeast	¾ teaspoon active dry yeast
3 tablespoons sugar	2 tablespoons sugar
2 teaspoons ground caraway (or caraway seeds)	1½ teaspoons ground caraway (or caraway seeds)
1½ tablespoons dry milk	1 tablespoon dry milk
½ cup rye flour	5 tablespoons rye flour
2½ cups bread flour	1½ cups + 2 tablespoons bread flour
1½ teaspoons salt	1 teaspoon salt
1½ tablespoons butter	1 tablespoon butter
9 ounces warm water	5½ ounces warm water

Note: For Panasonic/National machines, use 2 teaspoons of yeast for the 1½-pound loaf.

Nutritional Analysis

	1½-pound	1-pound	
Total calories	1785	1162	calories
Total protein	55	36	grams
Total carbohydrates	336	218	grams
Total fat	25	17	grams
Total saturated fat	12	8	grams
Total cholesterol	48	32	milligrams
Total sodium	3254	2169	milligrams
Total fibre	7	5	grams
Calories from fat	13	13	percent

Sheepherder's Bread

This is a favorite of many of my testers, especially those who like French breads. The recipe is simple but tasty, like those used by sheepherders in days of old. Time this bread to be done right before dinner; then tear it apart, rather than slice it, while still hot. Note that all-purpose flour is used to give it an authentic texture.

1½-pound	1-pound
1½ teaspoons active dry yeast	1 teaspoon active dry yeast
2 tablespoons sugar	4 teaspoons sugar
3 cups all-purpose flour	2 cups all-purpose flour
1 teaspoon salt	½ teaspoon salt
2½ tablespoons butter	1½ tablespoons butter
1 cup warm water	5½ ounces warm water

Note: For Panasonic/National machines, use 2 teaspoons of yeast for the 1½-pound loaf.

Nutritional Analysis

	1½-pound	1-pound	
Total calories	1838	1208	calories
Total protein	51	34	grams
Total carbohydrates	323	216	grams
Total fat	36	22	grams
Total saturated fat	19	11	grams
Total cholesterol	78	47	milligrams
Total sodium	2142	1073	milligrams
Total fibre	7	4	grams
Calories from fat	17	16	percent

Ham-and-Cheese Bread

Real cheese and pieces of ham make this a tangy, tasty bread. It is very moist and rich. It's literally a sandwich in a loaf of bread.

1½-pound	1-pound
2 teaspoons active dry yeast	1½ teaspoons active dry yeast
3½ teaspoons sugar	2½ teaspoons sugar
¼ cup chopped ham pieces	3 tablespoons chopped ham pieces
½ cup grated Swiss cheese	¼ cup grated Swiss cheese
2½ tablespoons dehydrated, minced onion	5 teaspoons dehydrated, minced onion
¾ cup grated cheddar cheese	½ cup grated cheddar cheese
1½ teaspoons paprika	1 teaspoon paprika
2½ tablespoons grated Parmesan cheese	5 teaspoons grated Parmesan cheese
1 teaspoon dry mustard	½ teaspoon dry mustard
½ teaspoon salt	¼ teaspoon salt
2½ cups bread flour	1¾ cups bread flour
2½ tablespoons butter	5 teaspoons butter
7 ounces warm milk	4½ ounces warm milk

Notes
1. For Panasonic/National machines, use 3 teaspoons of yeast for the 1½-pound loaf.
2. This bread has a high liquid content, so the top may fall during baking.
3. Use a light crust setting. The crust will be somewhat darker than usual, due to the fresh cheese in the recipe.

Nutritional Analysis

	1½-pound	1-pound	
Total calories	2354	1585	calories
Total protein	97	64	grams
Total carbohydrates	290	202	grams
Total fat	89	57	grams

Total saturated fat	52	33	grams
Total cholesterol	237	150	milligrams
Total sodium	2698	2142	milligrams
Total fibre	7	5	grams
Calories from fat	34	33	percent

Buttermilk Bread

This is a rich bread with a slightly coarser texture than white bread. It is excellent for breakfast toast.

1½-pound	*1-pound*
1 teaspoon active dry yeast	½ teaspoon active dry yeast
1 tablespoon sugar	2 teaspoons sugar
3 cups bread flour	2 cups bread flour
2 teaspoons salt	1½ teaspoons salt
1 cup warm buttermilk	5 ounces warm buttermilk
3 tablespoons butter	2 tablespoons butter

Note: For Panasonic/National machines, use 2 teaspoons of yeast for the 1½-pound loaf.

Nutritional Analysis

	1½-pound	*1-pound*	
Total calories	1954	1297	calories
Total protein	61	40	grams
Total carbohydrates	326	216	grams
Total fat	43	29	grams
Total saturated fat	23	15	grams
Total cholesterol	114	75	milligrams
Total sodium	4430	3302	milligrams
Total fibre	6	4	grams
Calories from fat	20	20	percent

Sour-Cream Bread

Somewhat tangy with poppy seeds, this bread doesn't rise as much as traditional white breads. However, it is excellent for cold-cuts sandwiches.

1½-pound

1 teaspoon active dry yeast

2 tablespoons sugar

3 cups bread flour

1 tablespoon poppy seeds

1½ teaspoons salt

1 cup sour cream

1½ ounces warm water

1-pound

½ teaspoon active dry yeast

4 teaspoons sugar

2 cups bread flour

2 teaspoons poppy seeds

1 teaspoon salt

¾ cup sour cream

1 tablespoon warm water

Notes
1. For Panasonic/National machines, use 2 teaspoons of yeast for the 1½-pound loaf.
2. For DAK/Welbilt machines, use 2½ ounces of warm water in the 1½-pound loaf.

Nutritional Analysis

	1½-pound	*1-pound*	
Total calories	2122	1454	calories
Total protein	59	40	grams
Total carbohydrates	335	224	grams
Total fat	59	43	grams
Total saturated fat	31	23	grams
Total cholesterol	102	77	milligrams
Total sodium	3331	2231	milligrams
Total fibre	7	5	grams
Calories from fat	25	27	percent

Italian Bread

A French-bread lover's delight, this Italian bread is similar to most French breads except for the addition of olive oil, which adds to the flavor. Serve the bread hot, and tear it apart for authentic Italian eating. It is great with any Italian dish, including spaghetti and lasagna.

1½-pound	*1-pound*
1½ teaspoons active dry yeast	1 teaspoon active dry yeast
3 cups bread flour	2 cups bread flour
1½ teaspoons salt	1 teaspoon salt
1 cup warm water	5 ounces warm water
2 tablespoons olive oil	4 teaspoons olive oil

Notes
1. For Panasonic/National machines, use 3 teaspoons of yeast for the 1½-pound loaf.
2. If your machine has a French-bread setting, use it with this recipe for a more authentic crust.

Nutritional Analysis

	1½-pound	1-pound	
Total calories	1734	1155	calories
Total protein	51	34	grams
Total carbohydrates	300	200	grams
Total fat	34	23	grams
Total saturated fat	5	3	grams
Total cholesterol	0	0	milligrams
Total sodium	3206	2137	milligrams
Total fibre	7	4	grams
Calories from fat	18	18	percent

Sally Lunn Bread

The origins of the name of this bread are unclear, but it is a rich variation on the white-bread theme with egg and extra sugar. It makes a rich sandwich bread and is excellent for toast. Sally Lunn is a high riser.

1½-pound	*1-pound*
1 teaspoon active dry yeast	½ teaspoon active dry yeast
4 tablespoons sugar	3 tablespoons sugar
3 cups bread flour	2 cups bread flour
1 teaspoon salt	½ teaspoon salt
5 ounces warm milk	3½ ounces warm milk
2 eggs	1 egg
5½ tablespoons butter	3½ tablespoons butter
½ cup warm water	1½ ounces warm water

Note: For Panasonic/National machines, use 2 teaspoons of yeast for the 1½-pound loaf.

Nutritional Analysis

	1½-pound	*1-pound*	
Total calories	2440	1601	calories
Total protein	68	43	grams
Total carbohydrates	355	241	grams
Total fat	81	51	grams
Total saturated fat	44	28	grams
Total cholesterol	603	326	milligrams
Total sodium	2348	1191	milligrams
Total fibre	6	4	grams
Calories from fat	30	28	percent

Picnic Bread

Picnic bread is fun for cold-cuts sandwiches because it already contains relish! This bread has a sweet and spicy taste and slightly yellow color. It looks and tastes great.

1½-pound	1-pound
1½ teaspoons active dry yeast	1 teaspoon active dry yeast
2 tablespoons sugar	1½ tablespoons sugar
3 cups bread flour	2 cups bread flour
1½ teaspoons salt	1 teaspoon salt
¼ cup sweet pickle relish (drained)	2 tablespoons sweet pickle relish (drained)
1½ tablespoons butter	1 tablespoon butter
6½ ounces warm milk	½ cup warm milk
3 tablespoons warm water	2 tablespoons warm water

Note: For Panasonic/National machines, use 2½ teaspoons of yeast for the 1½-pound loaf.

Nutritional Analysis

	1½-pound	1-pound	
Total calories	1904	1259	calories
Total protein	58	38	grams
Total carbohydrates	353	234	grams
Total fat	27	18	grams
Total saturated fat	13	9	grams
Total cholesterol	55	36	milligrams
Total sodium	3735	2414	milligrams
Total fibre	7	4	grams
Calories from fat	13	13	percent

WHOLE-GRAIN BREADS

The breads in this section are characterized by the use of whole-grain flours of all types. These tasty breads are among the most nutritious you can bake. If you purchased your bread machine to make healthful breads, take a close look at the recipes in this section.

Whole-Wheat Bread

In this recipe, half of the flour is bread flour while the other half is whole-wheat; That's what gives this bread a rich wheat taste as well as the cakier texture of white bread. It is an excellent and healthy whole-wheat bread.

1½-pound	*1-pound*
1½ teaspoons active dry yeast	1 teaspoon active dry yeast
1 tablespoon dough enhancer (optional)	1½ teaspoons dough enhancer (optional)
3 tablespoons sugar	2 tablespoons sugar
1½ tablespoons dry milk	1 tablespoon dry milk
1½ cups whole-wheat flour	1 cup whole-wheat flour
1½ cups bread flour	1 cup bread flour
1½ teaspoons salt	1 teaspoon salt
1½ tablespoons butter	1 tablespoon butter
9 ounces warm water	6 ounces warm water

Note: For Panasonic/National machines, use 2½ teaspoons of yeast for the 1½-pound loaf.

Nutritional Analysis

	1½-pound	*1-pound*	
Total calories	1682	1121	calories
Total protein	54	36	grams
Total carbohydrates	321	214	grams
Total fat	24	16	grams
Total saturated fat	12	8	grams
Total cholesterol	48	32	milligrams
Total sodium	3253	2168	milligrams
Total fibre	26	18	grams
Calories from fat	13	13	percent

Seven-Grain Bread

This bread is one of my family's favorites because of its crunchy texture and 100-percent wheat flavor. The addition of the dough enhancer will give the bread a smoother texture, but it is excellent either way.

1½-pound	1-pound
3 teaspoons active dry yeast	2 teaspoons active dry yeast
1 tablespoon dough enhancer (optional)	2 teaspoons dough enhancer (optional)
3 cups whole-wheat flour	2 cups whole-wheat flour
2 eggs	1 egg
1 teaspoon salt	½ teaspoon salt
½ cup seven-grain cereal	5 tablespoons seven-grain cereal
4 tablespoons honey	3 tablespoons honey
3 tablespoons olive oil	2 tablespoons olive oil
1 cup warm water	5 ounces warm water

Note: Soak the seven-grain cereal in the water for 30–60 minutes before adding to recipe.

Nutritional Analysis

	1½-pound	1-pound	
Total calories	2149	1421	calories
Total protein	71	45	grams
Total carbohydrates	356	242	grams
Total fat	59	38	grams
Total saturated fat	10	6	grams
Total cholesterol	426	213	milligrams
Total sodium	2265	1134	milligrams
Total fibre	53	35	grams
Calories from fat	25	24	percent

Tri-Grain Bread

A hearty combination of barley, oats, and wheat makes this bread an excellent choice for breakfast toast or sandwiches. It has a strong grain flavor and is a whole-grain lover's delight.

1½-pound	1-pound
1 tablespoon active dry yeast	2 teaspoons active dry yeast
1 tablespoon dough enhancer (optional)	2 teaspoons dough enhancer (optional)
1½ teaspoons gluten (optional)	1 teaspoon gluten (optional)
2¼ cups bread flour	1½ cups bread flour
4½ tablespoons oat flour	3 tablespoons oat flour
¼ cup barley flour	5 teaspoons barley flour
5 tablespoons wheat germ	3 tablespoons wheat germ
1½ teaspoons salt	1 teaspoon salt
3 teaspoons brown sugar	2 teaspoons brown sugar
2 tablespoons butter	1½ tablespoons butter
1 cup warm water	5 ounces warm water

Notes
1. For Panasonic/National machines, use 3½ teaspoons of yeast for the 1½-pound loaf.
2. For DAK/Welbilt machines, add 2 extra tablespoons (1 ounce) of water for the 1½-pound loaf.

Nutritional Analysis

	1½-pound	1-pound	
Total calories	1728	1203	calories
Total protein	59	38	grams
Total carbohydrates	302	213	grams
Total fat	34	24	grams
Total saturated fat	15	11	grams
Total cholesterol	62	47	milligrams
Total sodium	3216	2149	milligrams
Total fibre	18	11	grams
Calories from fat	18	18	percent

Whole-Wheat Three-Seed Bread

The three seeds (poppy, sunflower, and sesame) give a nutty flavor to this crunchy wheat-and-oatmeal bread. It's great for appetizer sandwiches. If you like seeds, you'll love this bread.

1½-pound	1-pound
2 teaspoons active dry yeast	1½ teaspoons active dry yeast
2 teaspoons gluten (optional)	1½ teaspoons gluten (optional)
2 tablespoons sunflower seeds	4 teaspoons sunflower seeds
2 tablespoons sesame seeds	4 teaspoons sesame seeds
2 tablespoons poppy seeds	4 teaspoons poppy seeds
½ cup rolled oats	¼ cup rolled oats
1 teaspoon salt	½ teaspoon salt
2 cups whole-wheat flour	1½ cups whole-wheat flour
3 tablespoons olive oil	2 tablespoons olive oil
2 tablespoons honey	4 teaspoons honey
1 cup warm water	5½ ounces warm water

Notes
1. For Panasonic/National machines, use 3 teaspoons of yeast for the 1½-pound loaf.
2. Note that this bread has a slightly higher liquid content than other recipes. If you would like a stiffer, drier bread, add 2 extra tablespoons of whole-wheat flour.

Nutritional Analysis

	1½-pound	1-pound	
Total calories	1748	1208	calories
Total protein	51	36	grams
Total carbohydrates	247	175	grams
Total fat	72	48	grams
Total saturated fat	9	6	grams
Total cholesterol	0	0	milligrams
Total sodium	2147	1076	milligrams
Total fibre	37	27	grams
Calories from fat	37	36	percent

100% Wheat Bread

This recipe is one of the best I have tasted. It captures the essence of whole-grain bread with its rich wheat flavor and its somewhat crumbly texture. Spread honey on a toasted slice for an unbelievable taste treat.

1½-pound	*1-pound*
4 teaspoons active dry yeast	2½ teaspoons active dry yeast
3 tablespoons honey	2 tablespoons honey
3 cups whole-wheat flour	2 cups whole-wheat flour
2 teaspoons salt	1½ teaspoons salt
¼ cup + 2 tablespoons wheat gluten	¼ cup wheat gluten
1½ cups warm water	1 cup warm water

Notes
1. For Panasonic/National machines, use 4 teaspoons of yeast for the 1½-pound loaf.
2. You will notice that the dough seems a little more liquid than usual. That is normal for this recipe, and the amount of liquid will yield a moist loaf. If the loaf collapses in your machine, cut back the liquid slightly (1 ounce or so) on the next try.

Nutritional Analysis

	1½-pound	*1-pound*	
Total calories	1729	1152	calories
Total protein	98	65	grams
Total carbohydrates	340	226	grams
Total fat	10	7	grams
Total saturated fat	1	1	grams
Total cholesterol	0	0	milligrams
Total sodium	4275	3205	milligrams
Total fibre	50	33	grams
Calories from fat	5	5	percent

German Rye Bread

If you like rye bread, you will love this authentic German country rye. Like all ryes, it has a dense texture and the distinctive taste of rye and caraway.

1½-pound	1-pound
1 tablespoon active dry yeast	2 teaspoons active dry yeast
1 tablespoon caraway seeds	2 teaspoons caraway seeds
2¼ cups bread flour	1½ cups bread flour
1½ teaspoons salt	1 teaspoon salt
2½ tablespoons unsweetened cocoa	5 teaspoons unsweetened cocoa
1½ cups rye flour	1 cup rye flour
1¼ cups warm water	7 ounces warm water
1½ tablespoons butter	1 tablespoon butter
2½ tablespoons molasses	5 teaspoons molasses

Note: For Panasonic/National machines, use 3½ teaspoons of yeast for the 1½-pound loaf.

Nutritional Analysis

	1½-pound	1-pound	
Total calories	2136	1423	calories
Total protein	72	48	grams
Total carbohydrates	403	269	grams
Total fat	30	20	grams
Total saturated fat	12	8	grams
Total cholesterol	47	31	milligrams
Total sodium	3250	2167	milligrams
Total fibre	10	6	grams
Calories from fat	13	13	percent

Corn Rye Bread

A must for rye lovers, Corn Rye is a wonderful, light variation of rye bread with the crunchiness of corn and the flavor of rye, wheat, and caraway.

1½-pound	*1-pound*
1½ teaspoons active dry yeast	1 teaspoon active dry yeast
1 teaspoon dough enhancer (optional)	½ teaspoon dough enhancer (optional)
2 teaspoons caraway seeds	1½ teaspoons caraway seeds
2½ tablespoons sesame seeds	5 teaspoons sesame seeds
¼ cup rye flour	2 tablespoons rye flour
¼ cup cornmeal	2 tablespoons cornmeal
2½ cups whole-wheat flour	1¾ cups whole-wheat flour
½ teaspoon salt	¼ teaspoon salt
2 teaspoons olive oil	1½ teaspoons olive oil
2 teaspoons molasses	1½ teaspoons molasses
1 cup warm water	¾ cup warm water

Notes
1. For Panasonic/National machines, use 2½ teaspoons of yeast for the 1½-pound loaf.
2. For DAK/Welbilt machines, add 2 tablespoons (1 ounce) of warm water to the 1½-pound recipe.

Nutritional Analysis

	1½-pound	*1-pound*	
Total calories	1506	1013	calories
Total protein	54	36	grams
Total carbohydrates	281	188	grams
Total fat	28	20	grams
Total saturated fat	4	3	grams
Total cholesterol	0	0	milligrams
Total sodium	1094	551	milligrams
Total fibre	44	30	grams
Calories from fat	17	17	percent

Swedish Limpa Rye Bread

A traditional Swedish favorite, this bread gets its distinctive flavor from the combination of molasses, orange, and rye. It is a heavy, dense bread. Don't look for it to rise much, but it will have a wonderful rye texture and flavor.

1½-pound	1-pound
3½ teaspoons active dry yeast	2½ teaspoons active dry yeast
1 cup rye flour	¾ cup rye flour
2 cups bread flour	1¼ cups bread flour
2 teaspoons grated orange peel	1½ teaspoons grated orange peel
2 teaspoons salt	1½ teaspoons salt
3½ tablespoons sugar	2½ tablespoons sugar
1 tablespoon butter	½ tablespoon butter
2 tablespoons molasses	4 teaspoons molasses
1 cup warm water	5½ ounces warm water

Note: For Panasonic/National machines, use 4 teaspoons of yeast for the 1½-pound loaf.

Nutritional Analysis

	1½-pound	1-pound	
Total calories	1811	1192	calories
Total protein	54	37	grams
Total carbohydrates	360	241	grams
Total fat	20	11	grams
Total saturated fat	8	4	grams
Total cholesterol	31	16	milligrams
Total sodium	4306	3226	milligrams
Total fibre	7	5	grams
Calories from fat	10	9	percent

Oatmeal Bread

This is a soft, rich-tasting oatmeal bread. Try a toasted slice with a bowl of hot oatmeal for a real oat lover's treat.

1½-pound	*1-pound*
1 teaspoon active dry yeast	¾ teaspoon active dry yeast
1 tablespoon dough enhancer (optional)	2 teaspoons dough enhancer (optional)
1½ tablespoons brown sugar	1 tablespoon brown sugar
1¼ cups rolled oats	¾ cup rolled oats
2¼ cups bread flour	1½ cups bread flour
1 teaspoon salt	½ teaspoon salt
4 teaspoons milk	2½ teaspoons milk
1½ tablespoons butter	1 tablespoon butter
1½ tablespoons molasses	1 tablespoon molasses
9 ounces warm water	¾ cup warm water

Note: For Panasonic/National machines, use 2 teaspoons of yeast for the 1½-pound loaf.

Nutritional Analysis

	1½-pound	*1-pound*	
Total calories	1834	1197	calories
Total protein	55	36	grams
Total carbohydrates	334	218	grams
Total fat	29	19	grams
Total saturated fat	13	8	grams
Total cholesterol	47	32	milligrams
Total sodium	2182	1098	milligrams
Total fibre	15	10	grams
Calories from fat	14	14	percent

Quinoa Bread

The nutty flavor of quinoa flour is evident in this high-protein loaf.
Quinoa is the grain of the ancient Incas and has been a staple in South
America for centuries. It has one of the highest protein contents of any
of the grains.

1½-pound	1-pound
1½ teaspoons active dry yeast	1 teaspoon active dry yeast
1½ tablespoons dry milk	1 tablespoon dry milk
3 tablespoons sugar	2 tablespoons sugar
1½ teaspoons salt	1 teaspoon salt
½ cup quinoa flour	¼ cup quinoa flour
½ cup whole-wheat flour	¼ cup whole-wheat flour
2 cups bread flour	1½ cups bread flour
1½ tablespoons butter	1 tablespoon butter
9 ounces warm water	¾ cup warm water

Note: For Panasonic/National machines, use 2 teaspoons of yeast for
the 1½-pound loaf.

Nutritional Analysis

	1½-pound	1-pound	
Total calories	1841	1223	calories
Total protein	57	37	grams
Total carbohydrates	342	228	grams
Total fat	28	18	grams
Total saturated fat	12	8	grams
Total cholesterol	48	32	milligrams
Total sodium	3253	2169	milligrams
Total fibre	12	7	grams
Calories from fat	14	13	percent

Buckwheat-Barley Bread

This bread features the distinctive tastes of barley and buckwheat. It is a light whole-grain bread with a texture approaching that of white bread. Try making a tuna sandwich with it or having it with chicken soup.

1½-pound

1½ teaspoons active dry yeast

1 tablespoon dough enhancer (optional)

¾ cup buckwheat flour

1½ tablespoons dry milk

3 tablespoons sugar

1½ teaspoons salt

¾ cup barley flour

1½ cups + 3 tablespoons bread flour

1½ tablespoons butter

9 ounces warm water

1-pound

1 teaspoon active dry yeast

2 teaspoons dough enhancer (optional)

½ cup buckwheat flour

1 tablespoon dry milk

2 tablespoons sugar

1 teaspoon salt

½ cup barley flour

1 cup + 2 tablespoons bread flour

1 tablespoon butter

¾ cup warm water

Note: For Panasonic/National machines, use 2 teaspoons of yeast for the 1½-pound loaf.

Nutritional Analysis

	1½-pound	1-pound	
Total calories	1766	1227	calories
Total protein	54	37	grams
Total carbohydrates	325	229	grams
Total fat	25	17	grams
Total saturated fat	12	8	grams
Total cholesterol	48	32	milligrams
Total sodium	3253	2169	milligrams
Total fibre	15	10	grams
Calories from fat	13	12	percent

Grape-Nuts Bread

Take one of your favorite breakfast cereals and make bread with it. It comes out with a wonderful nutty taste and great crunchy texture. Have it for breakfast along with your bowl of Grape-Nuts.

1½-pound

1½ teaspoons active dry yeast

1 tablespoon dough enhancer (optional)

½ cup Grape-Nuts cereal

1½ tablespoons dry milk

3 tablespoons sugar

1½ teaspoons salt

1¼ cups whole-wheat flour

1½ cups bread flour

1½ tablespoons butter

9 ounces warm water

1-pound

1 teaspoon active dry yeast

2 teaspoons dough enhancer (optional)

¼ cup Grape-Nuts cereal

1 tablespoon dry milk

2 tablespoons sugar

1 teaspoon salt

¾ cup whole-wheat flour

1 cup bread flour

1 tablespoon butter

¾ cup warm water

Note: For Panasonic/National machines, use 2 teaspoons of yeast for the 1½-pound loaf.

Nutritional Analysis

	1½-pound	1-pound	
Total calories	1800	1130	calories
Total protein	56	35	grams
Total carbohydrates	345	215	grams
Total fat	24	15	grams
Total saturated fat	12	8	grams
Total cholesterol	48	32	milligrams
Total sodium	3593	2338	milligrams
Total fibre	28	17	grams
Calories from fat	12	12	percent

Shredded-Wheat Bread

This is a whole-wheat bread with an interesting flavor and a crunch to it. Wheat lovers will eat this bread toasted with their morning bowl of shredded wheat.

1½-pound

1½ teaspoons active dry yeast

3 tablespoons sugar

1 tablespoon dough enhancer (optional)

½ cup shredded wheat (about 2 large biscuits)

1½ tablespoons dry milk

1½ teaspoons salt

1¼ cups whole-wheat flour

1¾ cups bread flour

1½ tablespoons butter

9 ounces warm water

1-pound

1 teaspoon active dry yeast

2 tablespoons sugar

½ tablespoon dough enhancer (optional)

½ cup shredded wheat (about 2 large biscuits)

1 tablespoon dry milk

1 teaspoon salt

¾ cup whole-wheat flour

1¼ cups bread flour

1 tablespoon butter

¾ cup warm water

Notes
1. For Panasonic/National machines, use 3 teaspoons of yeast for the 1½-pound loaf.
2. For DAK/Welbilt machines, use 11 ounces of warm water for the 1½-pound loaf.

Nutritional Analysis

	1½-pound	1-pound	
Total calories	1794	1233	calories
Total protein	56	38	grams
Total carbohydrates	343	236	grams
Total fat	25	17	grams
Total saturated fat	12	8	grams
Total cholesterol	48	32	milligrams
Total sodium	3253	2169	milligrams
Total fibre	23	14	grams
Calories from fat	13	12	percent

Cracked-Wheat Bread

The crunchy, light texture of this wheat favorite makes this an excellent bread to accompany soups and salads.

1½-pound

1½ teaspoons active dry yeast

1 cup whole-wheat flour

2 cups bread flour

1 teaspoon salt

½ cup cracked wheat

2 eggs

4 tablespoons honey

3 tablespoons olive oil

1 cup warm water

1-pound

1 teaspoon active dry yeast

¾ cup whole-wheat flour

1¼ cups bread flour

½ teaspoon salt

¼ cup cracked wheat

1 egg

2½ tablespoons honey

2 tablespoons olive oil

5 ounces warm water

Notes
1. For Panasonic/National machines, use 3 teaspoons of yeast for the 1½-pound loaf.
2. Combine the cracked wheat and water 1 hour before starting the bread.

Nutritional Analysis

	1½-pound	1-pound	
Total calories	2443	1538	calories
Total protein	75	46	grams
Total carbohydrates	416	263	grams
Total fat	59	37	grams
Total saturated fat	10	6	grams
Total cholesterol	426	213	milligrams
Total sodium	1201	1134	milligrams
Total fibre	23	16	grams
Calories from fat	22	22	percent

Russian Black Bread

This is a complete meal in a loaf. In fact, the story goes that during the siege of Leningrad, Russian black bread was all the Russians had to eat. It is nutritious and a must-try for rye lovers.

1½-pound	1-pound
2 teaspoons active dry yeast	1½ teaspoons active dry yeast
¼ teaspoon ground fennel seed	¼ teaspoon ground fennel seed
1 teaspoon dried onion	½ teaspoon dried onion
2 teaspoons ground caraway	1½ teaspoons ground caraway
¾ cup All-Bran cereal	½ cup All-Bran cereal
1 teaspoon salt	½ teaspoon salt
½ teaspoon sugar	½ teaspoon sugar
1 cup bread flour	¾ cup bread flour
1¼ cups rye flour	¾ cup rye flour
2 tablespoons butter	1½ tablespoons butter
1½ tablespoons unsweetened cocoa	1 tablespoon unsweetened cocoa
¼ cup molasses	2½ tablespoons molasses
1 tablespoon vinegar	2 teaspoons vinegar
¾ cup warm water	½ cup warm water

Note: For Panasonic/National machines, use 3½ teaspoons of yeast for the 1½-pound loaf.

Nutritional Analysis

	1½-pound	1-pound	
Total calories	1688	1146	calories
Total protein	53	36	grams
Total carbohydrates	326	218	grams
Total fat	34	24	grams
Total saturated fat	15	11	grams
Total cholesterol	62	47	milligrams
Total sodium	2788	1502	milligrams
Total fibre	29	19	grams
Calories from fat	18	19	percent

Sunflower-Nut Bread

This recipe combines sunflower seeds, nuts, whole wheat, and rolled oats, making a tangy-flavored light-textured bread. For extra crunchiness, add the seeds and nuts after the first rise instead of with the rest of the ingredients.

1½-pound	1-pound
2 teaspoons active dry yeast	1½ teaspoons active dry yeast
2 tablespoons sunflower seeds	4 teaspoons sunflower seeds
2 tablespoons chopped nuts	4 teaspoons chopped nuts
½ cup rolled oats	½ cup rolled oats
½ cup whole-wheat flour	½ cup whole-wheat flour
1 teaspoon salt	½ teaspoon salt
1 tablespoon brown sugar	2 teaspoons brown sugar
2 cups bread flour	1½ cups bread flour
4 teaspoons olive oil	1 tablespoon olive oil
½ cup warm water	3 ounces warm water
1½ tablespoons butter	1 tablespoon butter
5 ounces warm milk	3½ ounces warm milk

Notes
1. For Panasonic/National machines, use 3½ teaspoons of yeast for the 1½-pound loaf.
2. For DAK/Welbilt machines, use 5 ounces of warm water for the 1½-pound loaf.

Nutritional Analysis

	1½-pound	1-pound	
Total calories	1975	1412	calories
Total protein	60	44	grams
Total carbohydrates	298	215	grams
Total fat	62	44	grams
Total saturated fat	17	12	grams
Total cholesterol	53	35	milligrams
Total sodium	2225	1131	milligrams
Total fibre	18	15	grams
Calories from fat	28	28	percent

Onion Rye Bread

The taste of toasted onion combined with rye made this bread the favorite of my rye-loving bread testers. It makes an excellent bread for a ham-and-cheese sandwich.

1½-pound

1½ teaspoons active dry yeast

1 teaspoon caraway seeds

1 cup bread flour

3 tablespoons onion soup mix

1 cup rye flour

1 cup whole-wheat flour

1 tablespoon butter

2 tablespoons milk

1 tablespoon olive oil

1 tablespoon vinegar

2 teaspoons molasses

7 ounces warm water

1-pound

1 teaspoon active dry yeast

1 teaspoon caraway seeds

¾ cup bread flour

2 tablespoons onion soup mix

¾ cup rye flour

½ cup whole-wheat flour

1 tablespoon butter

4 teaspoons milk

2 teaspoons olive oil

2 teaspoons vinegar

1½ teaspoons molasses

4½ ounces warm water

Note: For Panasonic/National machines, use 3 teaspoons of yeast for the 1½-pound loaf.

Nutritional Analysis

	1½-pound	1-pound	
Total calories	1696	1178	calories
Total protein	57	38	grams
Total carbohydrates	307	207	grams
Total fat	34	27	grams
Total saturated fat	10	9	grams
Total cholesterol	32	32	milligrams
Total sodium	2877	1920	milligrams
Total fibre	20	11	grams
Calories from fat	18	21	percent

Barley Bread

If you like the sweet taste of barley, you'll enjoy this bread's distinctive barley flavor. It is a light-colored bread, with good texture and a whole-grain taste, punctuated by a light sesame flavor.

1½-pound	1-pound
1½ teaspoons active dry yeast	1 teaspoon active dry yeast
1 tablespoon dough enhancer (optional)	2 teaspoons dough enhancer (optional)
2 teaspoons sesame seeds	1½ teaspoons sesame seeds
1½ tablespoons dry milk	1 tablespoon dry milk
3 tablespoons sugar	2 tablespoons sugar
1½ teaspoons salt	1 teaspoon salt
1 cup barley flour	¾ cup barley flour
2 cups bread flour	1¼ cups bread flour
1½ tablespoons butter	1 tablespoon butter
9 ounces warm water	¾ cup warm water

Notes
1. For Panasonic/National machines, use 3 teaspoons of yeast for the 1½-pound loaf.
2. For DAK/Welbilt machines, use 10 ounces of warm water for the 1½-pound loaf.

Nutritional Analysis

	1½-pound	1-pound	
Total calories	1754	1173	calories
Total protein	53	35	grams
Total carbohydrates	312	206	grams
Total fat	27	19	grams
Total saturated fat	12	8	grams
Total cholesterol	48	32	milligrams
Total sodium	3255	2170	milligrams
Total fibre	19	14	grams
Calories from fat	14	15	percent

Buckwheat Bread

This is the bread for buckwheat lovers. Because of its strong buckwheat flavor and texture, it is excellent with vegetable soups or for morning toast.

1½-pound

1½ teaspoons active dry yeast

1 tablespoon dough enhancer (optional)

1½ tablespoons dry milk

3 tablespoons sugar

1¾ cups + 2 tablespoons bread flour

1½ teaspoons salt

1 tablespoon wheat or oat bran

¼ cup wheat germ

1¼ cup buckwheat flour

1½ tablespoons butter

9 ounces warm water

1-pound

1 teaspoon active dry yeast

2 teaspoons dough enhancer (optional)

1 tablespoon dry milk

2 tablespoons sugar

1¼ cups bread flour

1 teaspoon salt

2 teaspoons wheat or oat bran

2 tablespoons wheat germ

¾ cup buckwheat flour

1 tablespoon butter

¾ cup warm water

Notes
1. For Panasonic/National machines, use 3 teaspoons of yeast for the 1½-pound loaf.
2. For DAK/Welbilt machines, use 10 ounces of warm water in the 1½-pound loaf.

Nutritional Analysis

	1½-pound	1-pound	
Total calories	1881	1207	calories
Total protein	65	41	grams
Total carbohydrates	353	226	grams
Total fat	30	19	grams
Total saturated fat	13	8	grams
Total cholesterol	48	32	milligrams
Total sodium	3254	2170	milligrams
Total fibre	8	5	grams
Calories from fat	14	14	percent

Oat-Bran Bread

In addition to its good flavor, oat bran has been proven to be one of the healthiest of bread ingredients. This bread is a fine addition to any breakfast table.

1½-pound	*1-pound*
1½ teaspoons active dry yeast	1 teaspoon active dry yeast
2 tablespoons dry milk	1½ tablespoons dry milk
4 tablespoons sugar	2½ tablespoons sugar
½ cup oat bran	¼ cup oat bran
1 cup oat flour	¾ cup oat flour
1½ teaspoons salt	1 teaspoon salt
1½ cups bread flour	1 cup bread flour
1½ tablespoons butter	1 tablespoon butter
9 ounces warm water	¾ cup warm water

Notes
1. For Panasonic/National machines, use 3 teaspoons of yeast for the 1½-pound loaf.
2. For DAK/Welbilt machines, use 10 ounces of warm water for the 1½-pound loaf.

Nutritional Analysis

	1½-pound	*1-pound*	
Total calories	1666	1117	calories
Total protein	53	35	grams
Total carbohydrates	315	211	grams
Total fat	26	17	grams
Total saturated fat	11	8	grams
Total cholesterol	49	33	milligrams
Total sodium	3270	2185	milligrams
Total fibre	27	18	grams
Calories from fat	14	14	percent

Multi-Grain Bread

This bread combines five types of whole-grain flours for a grain lover's delight. All of these grains together create a unique loaf with a distinctive, but elusive, flavor.

1½-pound	1-pound
3 teaspoons active dry yeast	2 teaspoons active dry yeast
1 tablespoon dough enhancer (optional)	2 teaspoons dough enhancer (optional)
1½ teaspoons gluten	1 teaspoon gluten
¼ cup buckwheat flour	2 tablespoons buckwheat flour
¼ cup whole-wheat flour	2 tablespoons whole-wheat flour
2 cups bread flour	1½ cups bread flour
¼ cup oat flour	2 tablespoons oat flour
¼ cup barley flour	2 tablespoons barley flour
3 tablespoons oat bran	2 tablespoons oat bran
2 tablespoons wheat germ	4 teaspoons wheat germ
1 teaspoon salt	½ teaspoon salt
1 tablespoon brown sugar	2 teaspoons brown sugar
2 tablespoons butter	1½ tablespoons butter
9 ounces warm water	¾ cup warm water

Notes
1. For Panasonic/National machines, use 3½ teaspoons of yeast for the 1½-pound loaf.
2. For DAK/Welbilt machines, use 10 ounces of warm water in the 1½-pound loaf.

Nutritional Analysis

	1½-pound	1-pound	
Total calories	1772	1227	calories
Total protein	61	42	grams
Total carbohydrates	313	214	grams
Total fat	33	24	grams
Total saturated fat	15	11	grams

Total cholesterol	62	47	milligrams
Total sodium	2149	1078	milligrams
Total fibre	20	12	grams
Calories from fat	17	18	percent

Whole-Wheat Bagel Bread

If you don't feel like making bagels but want the texture of bagels with the low-fat nutritional benefits, try this bread. It tastes like a bagel and is especially good sliced and toasted.

1½-pound	*1-pound*
1½ teaspoons active dry yeast	1 teaspoon active dry yeast
1½ teaspoons gluten	1 teaspoon gluten
3 cups whole-wheat flour	2 cups whole-wheat flour
2 teaspoons salt	1½ teaspoons salt
3 tablespoons honey	2 tablespoons honey
1 cup warm water	5½ ounces warm water

Note: For Panasonic/National machines, use 3 teaspoons of yeast for the 1½-pound loaf.

Nutritional Analysis

	1½-pound	*1-pound*	
Total calories	1437	1030	calories
Total protein	54	38	grams
Total carbohydrates	313	226	grams
Total fat	7	5	grams
Total saturated fat	1	1	grams
Total cholesterol	0	0	milligrams
Total sodium	4269	3202	milligrams
Total fibre	46	31	grams
Calories from fat	4	4	percent

Pumpernickel Bread

The traditional taste of pumpernickel is a favorite of rye-bread lovers. With its dense rye texture, this bread is excellent when sliced thin for deli-type sandwiches.

1½-pound	1-pound
2½ teaspoons active dry yeast	2 teaspoons active dry yeast
1½ cups bread flour	1 cup bread flour
1½ cups rye flour	1 cup rye flour
1½ teaspoons salt	1 teaspoon salt
1 tablespoon caraway seed	2 teaspoons caraway seed
1 tablespoon butter	1 tablespoon butter
4 tablespoons molasses	2½ tablespoons molasses
6½ ounces warm water	4½ ounces warm water

Notes
1. For Panasonic/National machines, use 4 teaspoons of yeast for the 1½-pound loaf.
2. For DAK/Welbilt machines, use 7½ ounces of warm water in the 1½-pound loaf.

Nutritional Analysis

	1½-pound	1-pound	
Total calories	1744	1188	calories
Total protein	55	37	grams
Total carbohydrates	343	226	grams
Total fat	21	18	grams
Total saturated fat	8	8	grams
Total cholesterol	31	31	milligrams
Total sodium	3268	2177	milligrams
Total fibre	8	5	grams
Calories from fat	11	14	percent

Oatmeal-Sesame Bread

I keep getting repeat requests for this one. It has the spongy texture of oatmeal bread with the nutty taste of sesame seeds. It's a great sandwich bread.

1½-pound	1-pound
1½ teaspoons active dry yeast	1 teaspoon active dry yeast
2¾ cups bread flour	1¾ cups bread flour
1 teaspoon salt	½ teaspoon salt
4 tablespoons brown sugar	2½ tablespoons brown sugar
8 tablespoons sesame seeds	5 tablespoons sesame seeds
6 tablespoons rolled oats	¼ cup rolled oats
2 tablespoons butter	1½ tablespoons butter
9 ounces warm water	¾ cup warm water

Note: For Panasonic/National machines, use 3 teaspoons of yeast for the 1½-pound loaf.

Nutritional Analysis

	1½-pound	1-pound	
Total calories	2308	1489	calories
Total protein	64	41	grams
Total carbohydrates	365	232	grams
Total fat	67	45	grams
Total saturated fat	20	14	grams
Total cholesterol	62	47	milligrams
Total sodium	2167	1088	milligrams
Total fibre	12	8	grams
Calories from fat	26	27	percent

SPICE AND SWEET BREADS

If you like a lot of different flavors in your breads, these recipes will appeal to you. The spice breads use many different types of spices and seasonings to give them unique flavors. The sweet breads combine natural sweeteners with other bread ingredients to give you bread that will satisfy your sweet tooth in a low-calorie and natural way.

Cumin Spice Bread

Cumin, a relative of oregano, is a common spice in most Mexican foods. This bread has a distinct cumin flavor while still possessing the wonderful texture and taste of whole-grain flours.

1½-pound	1-pound
3 teaspoons active dry yeast	2 teaspoons active dry yeast
2 teaspoons dried orange peel	1½ teaspoons dried orange peel
1 teaspoon sugar	1 teaspoon sugar
2 teaspoons cumin powder	1¼ teaspoons cumin powder
½ cup rye flour	½ cup rye flour
1 teaspoon salt	½ teaspoon salt
½ cup whole-wheat flour	½ cup whole-wheat flour
2 cups bread flour	1¼ cups bread flour
7 ounces warm milk	6 ounces warm milk
5 tablespoons honey	3 tablespoons + 1 teaspoon honey
3 tablespoons olive oil	2 tablespoons olive oil

Nutritional Analysis

	1½-pound	1-pound	
Total calories	2200	1583	calories
Total protein	61	46	grams
Total carbohydrates	385	281	grams
Total fat	51	35	grams
Total saturated fat	8	6	grams
Total cholesterol	9	8	milligrams
Total sodium	2257	1170	milligrams
Total fibre	14	12	grams
Calories from fat	21	20	percent

Dilly Bread

This is an old family favorite. The cottage cheese (I use low-fat) gives it a great texture and flavor that is perfect with a salad. Note that all-purpose flour is used to maintain the original texture.

1½-pound	1-pound
2½ teaspoons active dry yeast	1½ teaspoons active dry yeast
3 cups all-purpose flour	2 cups all-purpose flour
½ teaspoon baking soda	¼ teaspoon baking soda
1½ teaspoons salt	1 teaspoon salt
1½ tablespoons dill weed	1 tablespoon dill weed
2½ tablespoons sugar	1½ tablespoons sugar
2 tablespoons warm water	1 tablespoon warm water
3 eggs	2 eggs
1 cup cottage cheese	¾ cup cottage cheese

Note: For Panasonic/National machines, use 3½ teaspoons of yeast for the 1½-pound loaf.

Nutritional Analysis

	1½-pound	1-pound	
Total calories	2056	1379	calories
Total protein	100	69	grams
Total carbohydrates	343	227	grams
Total fat	26	18	grams
Total saturated fat	8	5	grams
Total cholesterol	669	449	milligrams
Total sodium	4425	3035	milligrams
Total fibre	7	5	grams
Calories from fat	11	12	percent

Peppy Cheese Bread

This bread has a snappy cheese flavor and is great for a ham or tuna sandwich. Cut it into small pieces for tasty and attractive appetizer sandwiches.

1½-pound	1-pound
1½ teaspoons active dry yeast	1 teaspoon active dry yeast
3 cups bread flour	2 cups bread flour
3 tablespoons Parmesan cheese	2 tablespoons Parmesan cheese
¼ cup grated Swiss cheese	2 tablespoons grated Swiss cheese
1½ teaspoons oregano	1 teaspoon oregano
¼ cup grated cheddar cheese	2 tablespoons grated cheddar cheese
3 tablespoons wheat germ	2 tablespoons wheat germ
4 teaspoons sugar	1 tablespoon sugar
1½ teaspoons Louisiana-style hot sauce	1 teaspoon Louisiana-style hot sauce
2½ tablespoons butter	1½ tablespoons butter
9 ounces warm water	¾ cup warm water

Notes
1. For Panasonic/National machines, use 2½ teaspoons of yeast for the 1½-pound loaf.
2. Because of the fresh cheese content, use a lighter crust setting.
3. Because of the wetter dough caused by the melting cheese, the top of the loaf may fall during baking. This will not affect the taste of the bread.
4. The fresh cheeses may be added at the mix cycle, if desired.

Nutritional Analysis

	1½-pound	1-pound	
Total calories	2162	1395	calories
Total protein	77	49	grams
Total carbohydrates	329	221	grams
Total fat	60	35	grams
Total saturated fat	33	19	grams

Total cholesterol	144	82	milligrams
Total sodium	747	444	milligrams
Total fibre	9	6	grams
Calories from fat	25	23	percent

Taco Bread

The cornmeal and taco seasoning in this bread actually give it the flavor of a taco. It goes great with hot Southwestern chili.

1½-pound	1-pound
1½ teaspoons active dry yeast	1 teaspoon active dry yeast
2 cups bread flour	1¼ cups bread flour
3 tablespoons taco seasoning	2 tablespoons taco seasoning
¼ cup whole-wheat flour	2 tablespoons whole-wheat flour
¾ cup cornmeal	½ cup cornmeal
1 teaspoon garlic salt	½ teaspoon garlic salt
2 tablespoons sugar	4 teaspoons sugar
1½ tablespoons olive oil	1 tablespoon olive oil
9 ounces warm water	¾ cup warm water

Note: For Panasonic/National machines, use 2½ teaspoons of yeast for the 1½-pound loaf.

Nutritional Analysis

	1½-pound	1-pound	
Total calories	1803	1254	calories
Total protein	47	32	grams
Total carbohydrates	337	236	grams
Total fat	30	21	grams
Total saturated fat	4	3	grams
Total cholesterol	0	0	milligrams
Total sodium	5740	3482	milligrams
Total fibre	18	15	grams
Calories from fat	15	15	percent

Cheddar-Parmesan Bread

Watch out here! This is a rich bread (due to the cheese content), and no butter is needed. Just pop this bread right in your mouth. It is an excellent bread for a ham sandwich (no cheese needed), and the flavor will remind you of Cheese-It crackers.

1½-pound	1-pound
2 teaspoons active dry yeast	1½ teaspoons active dry yeast
2½ cups bread flour	1¾ cups bread flour
2½ tablespoons dried minced onion	5 teaspoons dried minced onion
1¼ cups grated cheddar cheese	¾ cup grated cheddar cheese
1½ teaspoons paprika	1 teaspoon paprika
2½ tablespoons Parmesan cheese	5 teaspoons Parmesan cheese
1 teaspoon dry mustard	½ teaspoon dry mustard
½ teaspoon salt	½ teaspoon salt
3½ teaspoons sugar	2½ teaspoons sugar
2½ tablespoons butter	5 teaspoons butter
7 ounces warm milk	4½ ounces warm milk

Notes
1. For Panasonic/National machines, use 3 teaspoons of yeast for the 1½-pound loaf.
2. Use a light-crust setting, because the cheese content of this bread gives it a tendency to bake to a dark-brown crust.

Nutritional Analysis

	1½-pound	1-pound	
Total calories	2329	1556	calories
Total protein	93	61	grams
Total carbohydrates	289	202	grams
Total fat	89	56	grams
Total saturated fat	52	33	grams
Total cholesterol	245	153	milligrams
Total sodium	2296	1826	milligrams

Total fibre	7	5	grams
Calories from fat	34	32	percent

Italian Spice Bread

This bread is an excellent complement to spaghetti or lasagna. It has a rich garlic taste with plenty of Italian spices.

1½-pound	*1-pound*
2½ teaspoons active dry yeast	1½ teaspoons active dry yeast
3 cups bread flour	2 cups bread flour
¼ cup grated Parmesan cheese	2½ tablespoons grated Parmesan cheese
1 teaspoon garlic salt	½ teaspoon garlic salt
1 tablespoon Italian spice	2 teaspoons Italian spice
½ cup dry milk	3½ tablespoons dry milk
1½ teaspoons garlic powder	1 teaspoon garlic powder
1¼ cups warm water	7 ounces warm water
¼ cup olive oil	2½ tablespoons olive oil

Notes
1. For Panasonic/National machines, use 3½ teaspoons of yeast for the 1½-pound loaf.
2. If you would like less garlic, omit the garlic powder.

Nutritional Analysis

	1½-pound	*1-pound*	
Total calories	2243	1433	calories
Total protein	76	47	grams
Total carbohydrates	327	212	grams
Total fat	68	43	grams
Total saturated fat	12	8	grams
Total cholesterol	25	14	milligrams
Total sodium	2763	1414	milligrams
Total fibre	8	5	grams
Calories from fat	27	27	percent

Pizza Bread

I call this bread instant pizza. It contains all the major ingredients of pizza and has a great pizza taste. Kids (large and small) will love it.

1½-pound	1-pound
2 teaspoons active dry yeast	1 teaspoon active dry yeast
1½ tablespoons sugar	1 tablespoon sugar
3 cups bread flour	2 cups bread flour
½ cup chopped pepperoni	¼ cup chopped pepperoni
1 teaspoon dried onion	½ teaspoon dried onion
1 teaspoon garlic powder	½ teaspoon garlic powder
3 tablespoons dry milk	2 tablespoons dry milk
2 teaspoons pizza spice	1½ teaspoons pizza spice
2 tablespoons Parmesan cheese	4 teaspoons Parmesan cheese
1 teaspoon garlic salt	½ teaspoon garlic salt
3 tablespoons olive oil	2 tablespoons olive oil
¾ cup warm water	½ cup warm water
¼ cup + 2 tablespoons tomato sauce	¼ cup tomato sauce

Notes
1. For Panasonic/National machines, use 3½ teaspoons of yeast for the 1½-pound loaf.
2. If your machine has a mix cycle, add the pepperoni at the "add" beep. Otherwise, pepperoni should be added after the initial mix.

Nutritional Analysis

	1½-pound	1-pound	
Total calories	2369	1530	calories
Total protein	79	50	grams
Total carbohydrates	338	225	grams
Total fat	76	47	grams
Total saturated fat	8	6	grams
Total cholesterol	11	7	milligrams
Total sodium	2922	1588	milligrams

Total fibre	7	5	grams
Calories from fat	29	28	percent

Dill Wheat Bread

A whole-grain variation of dill bread, this has a 100-percent wheat texture and flavor. For an airier loaf, the gluten is recommended.

1½-pound	*1-pound*
3 teaspoons active dry yeast	2 teaspoons active dry yeast
1½ teaspoons dried onions	1 teaspoon dried onions
2½ teaspoons gluten (optional)	2 teaspoons gluten (optional)
3 cups whole-wheat flour	2 cups whole-wheat flour
¼ teaspoon baking soda	¼ teaspoon baking soda
1½ teaspoons salt	1 teaspoon salt
2 tablespoons dill weed	1½ teaspoons dill weed
1 egg	1 egg
2 tablespoons butter	1½ tablespoons butter
1 cup cottage cheese	½ cup cottage cheese
2 tablespoons honey	1½ tablespoons honey
	2 tablespoons warm milk

Note: For Panasonic/National machines, use 3½ teaspoons of yeast for the 1½-pound loaf.

Nutritional Analysis

	1½-pound	*1-pound*	
Total calories	1879	1262	calories
Total protein	89	56	grams
Total carbohydrates	315	209	grams
Total fat	39	29	grams
Total saturated fat	19	14	grams
Total cholesterol	305	275	milligrams
Total sodium	4303	2720	milligrams
Total fibre	47	32	grams
Calories from fat	19	20	percent

Herb Bread

If you like herbs and spices, you will love this bread. It combines small amounts of herbs for just the right flavor. If you have any left over, dry it, and use it for turkey stuffing.

1½-pound	*1-pound*
1 teaspoon active dry yeast	½ teaspoon active dry yeast
2 tablespoons sugar	4 teaspoons sugar
3 cups bread flour	2 cups bread flour
2 teaspoons celery seed	1½ teaspoons celery seed
1 teaspoon ground sage	½ teaspoon ground sage
½ teaspoon nutmeg	¼ teaspoon nutmeg
1½ teaspoons salt	1 teaspoon salt
1 teaspoon parsley	½ teaspoon parsley
1 egg	1 egg
¾ cup warm milk	½ cup warm milk
2 tablespoons butter	1½ tablespoons butter
2 ounces warm water	3 tablespoons warm water

Notes
1. For Panasonic/National machines, use 2 teaspoons of yeast for the 1½-pound loaf.
2. For DAK/Welbilt machines, use 3 ounces of warm water for the 1½-pound loaf.

Nutritional Analysis

	1½-pound	*1-pound*	
Total calories	1960	1347	calories
Total protein	64	44	grams
Total carbohydrates	335	223	grams
Total fat	38	29	grams
Total saturated fat	19	14	grams
Total cholesterol	283	265	milligrams
Total sodium	3369	2267	milligrams
Total fibre	7	5	grams
Calories from fat	18	19	percent

Pumpkin-Pie Bread

My kids eat this bread before it has a chance to cool off. It tastes like pumpkin pie and makes a great after-school treat.

1½-pound	1-pound
2 teaspoons active dry yeast	1½ teaspoons active dry yeast
9 tablespoons sugar	6 tablespoons sugar
½ teaspoon ginger	¼ teaspoon ginger
1 teaspoon cinnamon	½ teaspoon cinnamon
½ teaspoon dried lemon peel	¼ teaspoon dried lemon peel
¾ cup whole-wheat flour	½ cup whole-wheat flour
1 teaspoon salt	½ teaspoon salt
2¼ cups bread flour	1½ cups bread flour
¼ cup + 2 tablespoons canned pumpkin	¼ cup canned pumpkin
3 ounces orange juice	¼ cup orange juice
3 ounces warm water	¼ cup warm water
2 eggs	1 egg
1½ tablespoons butter	1 tablespoon butter

Notes
1. For Panasonic/National machines, use 3½ teaspoons of yeast for the 1½-pound loaf.
2. For DAK/Welbilt machines, use ½ cup warm water in the 1½-pound loaf.

Nutritional Analysis

	1½-pound	1-pound	
Total calories	2225	1458	calories
Total protein	66	42	grams
Total carbohydrates	419	279	grams
Total fat	35	21	grams
Total saturated fat	15	9	grams
Total cholesterol	473	244	milligrams
Total sodium	2269	1136	milligrams
Total fibre	17	11	grams
Calories from fat	14	13	percent

Yorkshire Spice Bread

Derived from an authentic recipe, this is a wonderful, sweet bread with raisins and cinnamon flavor. It is excellent bread for morning toast.

1½-pound

1½ teaspoons active dry yeast

½ teaspoon cinnamon

½ teaspoon nutmeg

1 tablespoon dried orange peel

¼ cup powdered sugar

2½ cups + 2 tablespoons bread flour

1 egg

2 tablespoons olive oil

2 tablespoons butter

½ tablespoon maple syrup (or pancake syrup)

¾ cup warm milk

½ cup raisins

1-pound

1 teaspoon active dry yeast

½ teaspoon cinnamon

½ teaspoon nutmeg

2 teaspoons dried orange peel

3 tablespoons powdered sugar

1¾ cups bread flour

1 egg

4 teaspoons olive oil

4 teaspoons butter

1 teaspoon maple syrup (or pancake syrup)

½ cup warm milk

¼ cup raisins

Notes
1. For Panasonic/National machines, use 3 teaspoons of yeast for the 1½-pound loaf.
2. For best results, use the mix cycle and add the raisins at the beep. If your machine does not have a mix cycle, add the raisins after the initial mixing cycle.

Nutritional Analysis

	1½-pound	1-pound	
Total calories	2266	1758	calories
Total protein	59	45	grams
Total carbohydrates	367	278	grams
Total fat	64	54	grams
Total saturated fat	22	17	grams
Total cholesterol	283	262	milligrams
Total sodium	179	175	milligrams
Total fibre	10	8	grams
Calories from fat	25	28	percent

Hawaiian Bread

This bread works well when you want a sweet substitute for white bread. It's great with jelly or jam.

1½-pound	1-pound
1½ teaspoons active dry yeast	1 teaspoon active dry yeast
5 tablespoons sugar	3 tablespoons sugar
3 cups bread flour	2 cups bread flour
½ teaspoon salt	½ teaspoon salt
2 tablespoons dry milk	4 teaspoons dry milk
2 tablespoons instant-mashed-potato flakes	4 teaspoons instant-mashed-potato flakes
¼ teaspoon lemon extract	¼ teaspoon lemon extract
¼ teaspoon vanilla extract	¼ teaspoon vanilla extract
2 eggs	1 egg
4 tablespoons butter	2½ tablespoons butter
1 cup warm water	5 ounces warm water

Note: For Panasonic/National machines, use 3 teaspoons of yeast for the 1½-pound loaf.

Nutritional Analysis

	1½-pound	1-pound	
Total calories	2351	1511	calories
Total protein	68	44	grams
Total carbohydrates	371	243	grams
Total fat	64	39	grams
Total saturated fat	33	20	grams
Total cholesterol	552	292	milligrams
Total sodium	1356	1238	milligrams
Total fibre	7	4	grams
Calories from fat	25	23	percent

Peanut-Butter-and-Jelly Bread

This is a fun bread. You can vary it by adding different types of jelly or jam each time you make it.

1½-pound

2 teaspoons active dry yeast

3½ tablespoons peanut butter

3 tablespoons jelly or jam

2½ cups bread flour

1½ teaspoons salt

2 tablespoons sugar

½ cup warm milk

½ cup warm water

1-pound

1½ teaspoons active dry yeast

2½ tablespoons peanut butter

2 tablespoons jelly or jam

1½ cups bread flour

1 teaspoon salt

3½ teaspoons sugar

¼ cup warm milk

2½ ounces warm water

Note: For Panasonic/National machines, use 3½ teaspoons of yeast for the 1½-pound loaf.

Nutritional Analysis

	1½-pound	*1-pound*	
Total calories	1886	1175	calories
Total protein	60	38	grams
Total carbohydrates	333	203	grams
Total fat	35	24	grams
Total saturated fat	7	5	grams
Total cholesterol	5	3	milligrams
Total sodium	3289	2183	milligrams
Total fibre	10	6	grams
Calories from fat	17	19	percent

Apple-Pie Bread

This is so much like the real thing that it even contains apple-pie filling. It is moist, tangy, and a great breakfast bread.

1½-pound

1½ teaspoons active dry yeast

1½ teaspoons cinnamon

5 tablespoons sugar

3¼ cups + 2 tablespoons bread flour

1½ teaspoons salt

3 tablespoons buttermilk powder or dry milk

¾ cup apple-pie filling

1½ tablespoons butter

4½ ounces apple juice

1-pound

1 teaspoon active dry yeast

1 teaspoon cinnamon

3½ tablespoons sugar

2¼ cups bread flour

1 teaspoon salt

4 teaspoons buttermilk powder or dry milk

½ cup apple-pie filling

1 tablespoon butter

3 ounces apple juice

Note: For Panasonic/National machines, use 3 teaspoons of yeast for the 1½-pound loaf.

Nutritional Analysis

	1½-pound	*1-pound*	
Total calories	2376	1591	calories
Total protein	62	42	grams
Total carbohydrates	468	314	grams
Total fat	26	17	grams
Total saturated fat	12	8	grams
Total cholesterol	57	38	milligrams
Total sodium	3382	2255	milligrams
Total fibre	9	6	grams
Calories from fat	10	10	percent

Onion French Bread

This is a delicious, low-fat French bread with an onion flavor. It is excellent with soup, salad, or Italian foods.

1½-pound

3 teaspoons active dry yeast

3 cups bread flour

1 package onion-soup mix

1¼ cups warm water

1-pound

2 teaspoons active dry yeast

2 cups bread flour

3 tablespoons onion-soup mix

7 ounces warm water

Notes
1. For Panasonic/National machines, use 3½ teaspoons of yeast for the 1½-pound loaf.
2. Use the "French bread" setting if your machine has one.

Nutritional Analysis

	1½-pound	*1-pound*	
Total calories	1656	1094	calories
Total protein	58	38	grams
Total carbohydrates	333	220	grams
Total fat	9	6	grams
Total saturated fat	1	1	grams
Total cholesterol	0	0	milligrams
Total sodium	4750	2851	milligrams
Total fibre	7	5	grams
Calories from fat	5	5	percent

FRUIT AND VEGETABLE BREADS

These recipes focus on the variety of flavors available using fruits and vegetables in breads. They vary greatly in their content and texture, but you will find that they all contain natural, nutritious ingredients that are sure to please your palate.

Cinnamon-Raisin-Nut Bread

Although not an extremely sweet bread, it is very flavorful. The nuts give it a great crunch, especially if added during the mix cycle.

1½-pound	*1-pound*
2 teaspoons active dry yeast	1½ teaspoons active dry yeast
3½ tablespoons sugar	2½ tablespoons sugar
2 cups bread flour	1½ cups bread flour
2 teaspoons dry milk	1½ teaspoons dry milk
1½ teaspoons cinnamon	1 teaspoon cinnamon
1 teaspoon salt	½ teaspoon salt
2½ tablespoons honey	1½ tablespoons honey
2 tablespoons butter	1½ tablespoons butter
1 egg	1 egg
3 tablespoons warm water	2 tablespoons warm water
3 ounces warm milk	2½ ounces warm milk
½ cup raisins	¼ cup raisins
½ cup chopped nuts	¼ cup chopped nuts

Notes
1. For Panasonic/National machines, use 3½ teaspoons of yeast for the 1½-pound loaf.
2. For DAK/Welbilt machines, use 5 tablespoons of warm water for the 1½-pound loaf.
3. For best results, add the raisins and chopped nuts after the first mixing. If your machine has a mix cycle, use it and add the raisins and nuts at the "mix" beep.

Nutritional Analysis

	1½-pound	*1-pound*	
Total calories	2253	1532	calories
Total protein	57	42	grams
Total carbohydrates	360	246	grams
Total fat	71	45	grams
Total saturated fat	20	15	grams
Total cholesterol	279	263	milligrams

Total sodium	2287	1198	milligrams
Total fibre	12	8	grams
Calories from fat	28	27	percent

Apple Bread

A very tangy, tart-tasting bread with low calories, it has a strong apple flavor. This bread goes great with pork chops or pork roast.

1½-pound

2½ teaspoons active dry yeast

4 tablespoons sugar

2½ cups bread flour

¼ teaspoon nutmeg

1 teaspoon cinnamon

½ teaspoon salt

½ cup whole-wheat flour

1 tablespoon butter

1 cup + 2 tablespoons apple sauce

1-pound

1½ teaspoons active dry yeast

2½ tablespoons sugar

1¾ cups bread flour

¼ teaspoon nutmeg

½ teaspoon cinnamon

¼ teaspoon salt

¼ cup whole-wheat flour

1 tablespoon butter

¾ cup apple sauce

Note: For Panasonic/National machines, use 3½ teaspoons of yeast for the 1½-pound loaf.

Nutritional Analysis

	1½-pound	*1-pound*	
Total calories	1864	1275	calories
Total protein	53	35	grams
Total carbohydrates	366	243	grams
Total fat	20	17	grams
Total saturated fat	8	8	grams
Total cholesterol	31	31	milligrams
Total sodium	1077	540	milligrams
Total fibre	14	8	grams
Calories from fat	10	12	percent

Whole-Wheat Oat Cinnamon Raisin Bread

This bread combines the great taste and texture of whole wheat with the nutrition of oats and raisins for a naturally sweet loaf.

1½-pound	1-pound
2 teaspoons active dry yeast	1½ teaspoons active dry yeast
2 teaspoons gluten (optional)	1½ teaspoons gluten (optional)
2 teaspoons dough enhancer (optional)	1½ teaspoons dough enhancer (optional)
2 cups whole-wheat flour	1½ cups whole-wheat flour
1 tablespoon cinnamon	2 teaspoons cinnamon
½ cup rolled oats	¼ cup rolled oats
1 teaspoon salt	1 teaspoon salt
2 tablespoons olive oil	4 teaspoons olive oil
2 tablespoons honey	4 teaspoons honey
1 cup warm water	5½ ounces warm water
¾ cup raisins	½ cup raisins

Notes
1. For Panasonic/National machines, use 3½ teaspoons of yeast for the 1½-pound loaf.
2. For best results, add the raisins at the end of the first mixing or use the mix cycle. If your machine has a mix cycle, add the raisins at the "mix" beep.

Nutritional Analysis

	1½-pound	1-pound	
Total calories	1685	1166	calories
Total protein	45	32	grams
Total carbohydrates	327	228	grams
Total fat	35	23	grams
Total saturated fat	5	3	grams
Total cholesterol	0	0	milligrams
Total sodium	2155	2147	milligrams
Total fibre	43	30	grams
Calories from fat	19	18	percent

Cranberry Bread

The tart, tangy flavor of cranberries is predominant in this light, pink bread. A slice is excellent with meat, especially poultry or pork.

1½-pound

1 teaspoon active dry yeast

¼ cup sugar

3 cups bread flour

2 teaspoons orange peel

½ teaspoon salt

½ cup canned cranberries

3 ounces warm water

1 tablespoon olive oil

3 ounces orange juice

1 egg

2 tablespoons chopped nuts

1-pound

½ teaspoon active dry yeast

2 tablespoons sugar

2 cups bread flour

1½ teaspoons orange peel

½ teaspoon salt

¼ cup canned cranberries

¼ cup warm water

2 teaspoons olive oil

¼ cup orange juice

1 egg

4 teaspoons chopped nuts

Notes
1. For Panasonic/National machines, use 3 teaspoons of yeast for the 1½-pound loaf.
2. Nuts are best added during the mix cycle, if your machine has one. If your machine does not have a mix cycle, you can either add the nuts at the beginning (with the rest of the ingredients) or after the initial mixing has taken place.

Nutritional Analysis

	1½-pound	*1-pound*	
Total calories	2098	1377	calories
Total protein	59	41	grams
Total carbohydrates	382	243	grams
Total fat	35	25	grams
Total saturated fat	5	4	grams
Total cholesterol	213	213	milligrams
Total sodium	1158	1145	milligrams
Total fibre	7	5	grams
Calories from fat	15	16	percent

Banana Oat-Bran Bread

This bread is nutritious and delicious, with a light banana flavor and a great oat texture.

1½-pound

2 teaspoons active dry yeast

2 bananas

2 cups bread flour

½ teaspoon salt

5 tablespoons oat bran

½ cup + 2 tablespoons oat flour

½ teaspoon vanilla

2 tablespoons olive oil

2 eggs

½ cup warm water

2½ tablespoons honey

1-pound

1½ teaspoons active dry yeast

1½ bananas

1½ cups bread flour

¼ teaspoon salt

3 tablespoons oat bran

¼ cup + 2½ tablespoons oat flour

½ teaspoon vanilla

4 teaspoons olive oil

2 eggs

3 ounces warm water

2 tablespoons honey

Note: For Panasonic/National machines, use 3 teaspoons of yeast for the 1½-pound loaf.

Nutritional Analysis

	1½-pound	*1-pound*	
Total calories	2103	1558	calories
Total protein	64	49	grams
Total carbohydrates	367	268	grams
Total fat	46	34	grams
Total saturated fat	8	6	grams
Total cholesterol	426	426	milligrams
Total sodium	1203	667	milligrams
Total fibre	23	15	grams
Calories from fat	20	20	percent

Apple-Butter Bread

This is a sweet bread with a distinct apple flavor, enhanced with nuts.

1½-pound	1-pound
2 teaspoons active dry yeast	1½ teaspoons active dry yeast
½ cup sugar	¼ cup sugar
1 teaspoon cinnamon	½ teaspoon cinnamon
3 cups bread flour	2 cups bread flour
½ teaspoon salt	¼ teaspoon salt
3 tablespoons warm water	2 tablespoons warm water
¾ cup apple butter	½ cup apple butter
1 egg	1 egg
1 teaspoon vanilla	½ teaspoon vanilla
3 tablespoons butter	2 tablespoons butter
½ cup chopped nuts	¼ cup chopped nuts

Note: For Panasonic/National machines, use 3½ teaspoons of yeast for the 1½-pound loaf.

Nutritional Analysis

	1½-pound	1-pound	
Total calories	2799	1767	calories
Total protein	67	45	grams
Total carbohydrates	445	280	grams
Total fat	84	51	grams
Total saturated fat	27	18	grams
Total cholesterol	306	275	milligrams
Total sodium	1178	628	milligrams
Total fibre	10	7	grams
Calories from fat	27	26	percent

Orange Bread

The light-orange color and aroma of this bread complement its distinctive orange flavor. It goes well with fruit salad, and it is great for breakfast toast.

1½-pound

1 teaspoon active dry yeast

3 cups bread flour

½ teaspoon salt

¼ cup + 1 tablespoon sugar

1 tablespoon orange peel

1 egg

2 tablespoons butter

3 ounces orange juice

¾ cup warm water

1-pound

½ teaspoon active dry yeast

2 cups bread flour

½ teaspoon salt

3 tablespoons sugar

2 teaspoons orange peel

1 egg

1½ tablespoons butter

¼ cup orange juice

½ cup warm water

Note: For Panasonic/National machines, use 2½ teaspoons of yeast for the 1½-pound loaf.

Nutritional Analysis

	1½-pound	*1-pound*	
Total calories	2039	1385	calories
Total protein	57	40	grams
Total carbohydrates	369	242	grams
Total fat	35	27	grams
Total saturated fat	17	13	grams
Total cholesterol	275	260	milligrams
Total sodium	1138	1135	milligrams
Total fibre	6	4	grams
Calories from fat	15	18	percent

Carrot-Celery Bread

The light taste of celery and carrots combined with whole wheat makes this a great sandwich bread, especially for cold cuts. Try it with a bacon-lettuce-tomato sandwich for a unique treat.

1½-pound	1-pound
1½ teaspoons active dry yeast	1 teaspoon active dry yeast
1½ cups whole-wheat flour	1 cup whole-wheat flour
1½ cups bread flour	1 cup bread flour
½ cup grated carrots	¼ cup grated carrots
1 teaspoon salt	½ teaspoon salt
1 teaspoon celery seed	½ teaspoon celery seed
1 tablespoon olive oil	2 teaspoons olive oil
2 tablespoons honey	1½ tablespoons honey
1 cup warm water	5½ ounces warm water

Note: For Panasonic/National machines, use 3 teaspoons of yeast for the 1½-pound loaf.

Nutritional Analysis

	1½-pound	1-pound	
Total calories	1635	1094	calories
Total protein	52	34	grams
Total carbohydrates	320	215	grams
Total fat	21	14	grams
Total saturated fat	3	2	grams
Total cholesterol	0	0	milligrams
Total sodium	2160	1081	milligrams
Total fibre	28	19	grams
Calories from fat	12	11	percent

Cheddar Olive Bread

Olives and cheese have always been a great combination, and they are both present in this tasty bread. This was one of the tasters' favorites.

1½-pound	1-pound
1½ teaspoons active dry yeast	1 teaspoon active dry yeast
3 cups bread flour	2 cups bread flour
4 teaspoons cornmeal	1 tablespoon cornmeal
1 teaspoon salt	½ teaspoon salt
1 teaspoon basil	½ teaspoon basil
1 tablespoon olive oil	2 teaspoons olive oil
2 eggs	1 egg
¾ cup warm water	½ cup warm water
½ cup sliced or grated black olives	¼ cup sliced or grated black olives
¾ cup grated cheddar cheese	½ cup grated cheddar cheese

Notes

1. For Panasonic/National machines, use 3 teaspoons of yeast for the 1½-pound loaf.
2. For DAK/Welbilt machines, use one extra tablespoon of warm water if the machine seems to labor with the 1½-pound loaf.
3. The dough will seem very stiff at first; however, once the cheese melts, the consistency will be about right.
4. For best results, add the olives during the mix cycle. If your machine does not have a mix cycle, add the olives after the initial mixing has completed.

Nutritional Analysis

	1½-pound	1-pound	
Total calories	2213	1441	calories
Total protein	86	55	grams
Total carbohydrates	314	209	grams
Total fat	66	41	grams
Total saturated fat	25	16	grams
Total cholesterol	515	273	milligrams
Total sodium	3393	1786	milligrams
Total fibre	10	6	grams
Calories from fat	27	26	percent

V-8 Bread

If you like tomato juice and V-8 juice, you'll like this bread. It uses V-8 juice as the liquid and combines that flavor with some seasonings to produce a light-orange bread with a distinctively vegetable taste.

1½-pound	1-pound
2 teaspoons active dry yeast	1½ teaspoons active dry yeast
1½ tablespoons sugar	1 tablespoon sugar
3 cups bread flour	2 cups bread flour
1 teaspoon dried onion	½ teaspoon dried onion
1 teaspoon garlic powder	½ teaspoon garlic powder
3 tablespoons dry milk	2 tablespoons dry milk
2 teaspoons Italian spice	1½ teaspoons Italian spice
2 tablespoons Parmesan cheese	1½ tablespoons Parmesan cheese
1 teaspoon garlic salt	½ teaspoon garlic salt
3 tablespoons olive oil	2 tablespoons olive oil
¼ cup warm water	¼ cup warm water
7 ounces V-8 juice	5 ounces V-8 juice

Notes
1. For Panasonic/National machines, use 3 teaspoons of yeast for the 1½-pound loaf.
2. If you like the taste but want to lower the salt content, buy salt-free V-8 juice and eliminate the garlic salt from the recipe.

Nutritional Analysis

	1½-pound	1-pound	
Total calories	2085	1396	calories
Total protein	63	42	grams
Total carbohydrates	339	227	grams
Total fat	51	34	grams
Total saturated fat	8	6	grams
Total cholesterol	11	8	milligrams
Total sodium	3084	1748	milligrams
Total fibre	7	5	grams
Calories from fat	22	22	percent

Carrot Bread

This bread is bright orange in color. It has all the nutrients and flavor of fresh carrots. Prepare the carrot puree by steaming or boiling them. Then liquefy them in your blender or food processor.

1½-pound	1-pound
1 teaspoon active dry yeast	½ teaspoon active dry yeast
1 tablespoon sugar	2 teaspoons sugar
3 cups bread flour	2 cups bread flour
½ teaspoon nutmeg	¼ teaspoon nutmeg
½ teaspoon salt	½ teaspoon salt
¾ cup carrot puree	½ cup carrot puree
1 egg	1 egg
2 tablespoons + 1 teaspoon butter	1½ tablespoons butter
3 tablespoons warm milk	2 tablespoons warm milk
1½ tablespoons warm water	1 tablespoon warm water

Notes
1. For Panasonic/National machines, use 2 teaspoons of yeast for the 1½-pound loaf.
2. Be sure not to add the carrot puree while it is still hot from steaming. Let it cool so that you don't kill the yeast.

Nutritional Analysis

	1½-pound	1-pound	
Total calories	1907	1289	calories
Total protein	59	41	grams
Total carbohydrates	323	215	grams
Total fat	40	27	grams
Total saturated fat	20	13	grams
Total cholesterol	287	261	milligrams
Total sodium	1190	1170	milligrams
Total fibre	9	6	grams
Calories from fat	19	19	percent

Sweet-Potato Bread

If you like yams on the dinner table, try this bread instead. It's a great supplement to a turkey dinner.

1½-pound	1-pound
1½ teaspoons active dry yeast	1 teaspoon active dry yeast
9 tablespoons brown sugar	6 tablespoons brown sugar
½ teaspoon ginger	¼ teaspoon ginger
3 cups bread flour	2 cups bread flour
1 teaspoon cinnamon	1 teaspoon cinnamon
½ teaspoon dried orange peel	½ teaspoon dried orange peel
1 teaspoon salt	½ teaspoon salt
¼ cup + 2 tablespoons canned yams	¼ cup canned yams
3 ounces orange juice	¼ cup orange juice
3 ounces warm water	¼ cup warm water
2 eggs	1 egg
1½ tablespoons butter	1 tablespoon butter

Note: For Panasonic/National machines, use 3 teaspoons of yeast for the 1½-pound loaf.

Nutritional Analysis

	1½-pound	1-pound	
Total calories	2359	1549	calories
Total protein	65	41	grams
Total carbohydrates	445	297	grams
Total fat	35	22	grams
Total saturated fat	15	9	grams
Total cholesterol	473	244	milligrams
Total sodium	2320	1171	milligrams
Total fibre	7	5	grams
Calories from fat	13	13	percent

Potato Bread

This is an old favorite, updated to use modern ingredients such as potato flakes. Still, the old-fashioned flavor persists, and this bread is great with soups.

1½-pound	*1-pound*
1 teaspoon active dry yeast	½ teaspoon active dry yeast
2 tablespoons sugar	4 teaspoons sugar
2¾ cups bread flour	2 cups bread flour
1 teaspoon salt	½ teaspoon salt
4 tablespoons instant-mashed-potato flakes	2½ tablespoons instant-mashed-potato flakes
¼ cup dry milk	2 tablespoons dry milk
½ cup buttermilk	2½ ounces buttermilk
2 eggs	1 egg
2 tablespoons butter	1 tablespoon butter
5 ounces warm water	3½ ounces warm water

Notes
1. For Panasonic/National machines, use 2 teaspoons of yeast for the 1½-pound loaf.
2. For DAK/Welbilt machines, use ¾ cup warm water for the 1½-pound loaf.

Nutritional Analysis

	1½-pound	*1-pound*	
Total calories	2073	1384	calories
Total protein	79	51	grams
Total carbohydrates	334	236	grams
Total fat	44	24	grams
Total saturated fat	19	10	grams
Total cholesterol	513	259	milligrams
Total sodium	2727	1407	milligrams
Total fibre	6	4	grams
Calories from fat	19	16	percent

Zucchini Bread

If one of your favorite summer vegetables is zucchini, here is a bread that will definitely have a place on your summer table.

1½-pound	1-pound
1½ teaspoons active dry yeast	1 teaspoon active dry yeast
1½ tablespoons brown sugar	1 tablespoon brown sugar
1¾ cups + 3 tablespoons bread flour	1¼ cups + 1 tablespoon bread flour
½ cup whole-wheat flour	½ cup whole-wheat flour
1 cup shredded zucchini	¾ cup shredded zucchini
1 teaspoon salt	½ teaspoon salt
1½ teaspoons ground coriander	1 teaspoon ground coriander
2½ tablespoons dry milk	1½ tablespoons dry milk
¼ cup wheat germ	2 tablespoons wheat germ
1½ tablespoons butter	1 tablespoon butter
5½ ounces warm water	3½ ounces warm water

Notes
1. For Panasonic/National machines, use 3 teaspoons of yeast for the 1½-pound loaf.
2. For DAK/Welbilt machines, use 6½ ounces of warm water in the 1½-pound recipe.

Nutritional Analysis

	1½-pound	1-pound	
Total calories	1580	1112	calories
Total protein	58	40	grams
Total carbohydrates	287	205	grams
Total fat	27	18	grams
Total saturated fat	12	8	grams
Total cholesterol	49	33	milligrams
Total sodium	2231	1127	milligrams
Total fibre	17	13	grams
Calories from fat	15	15	percent

SOURDOUGH BREADS

Sourdough is a pioneer tradition in this country, made famous during the gold-rush days in California. Miners had to make bread, but they couldn't maintain leavening of any kind. So, they made sourdough, a live mixture of fermenting bacteria that acted much like yeast. They kept their starter alive year after year (it really does get better with age) and used it daily for baking breads, biscuits, and pancakes.

All the recipes in this section use sourdough starter (see recipe on following page). Even with a bread machine, sourdough-bread recipes require a little more patience than other bread recipes because the sourdough batter must be prepared. Here is the procedure for making sourdough batter for your recipes:

1. Remove your sourdough starter from the refrigerator and allow it to reach room temperature (allow for about 6 hours).
2. Place 1½ cups of starter in a 2-quart mixing bowl.
3. Return the remaining starter to the refrigerator.
4. Add 1½ cups of all-purpose flour and 1 cup of warm skim milk and mix well. The batter should have the consistency of a light pancake batter.
5. Cover the bowl lightly and let the batter proof for 8–12 hours in an 85–90 degree environment.
6. After proofing, use what batter you need for your bread (it can remain out for 1–3 days), but make sure you save at least 1½ cups of batter to replenish your starter.
7. Return the remaining batter to your starter pot. Stir and refrigerate.

Many people will place the starter directly into the ingredients. While this method will certainly work, it is not the best way to keep the starter active, because after you remove the starter, you have to add flour and milk and again proof the starter.

I have found it better to use the batter method described above. It tends to keep my starter more active and gives me plenty of batter to use in my recipes. If you use the batter method, place batter in the recipe any time sourdough starter is called for.

Sourdough Starter

This recipe will give you enough starter to begin with. Each time you remove starter to make batter, don't forget to replenish the starter with the leftover batter.

1. Warm a quart jar or similar container by filling it with hot tap water and letting it sit for a few minutes.

2. In a pan or microwave oven, heat 1 cup skim or low-fat milk to 100–110 degrees. Then, remove it from the heat and add 3 tablespoons of plain yogurt to the mix.

3. Drain the warm water from the jar and wipe it dry.

4. Pour the milk-yogurt mixture into the jar and cover. Note that it is preferable to use a plastic lid, but if your jar has a metal lid, place plastic wrap or waxed paper under the lid before screwing it tight.

5. Place the mixture in a warm place, and allow it to proof for 24 hours.

6. Stir 1 cup of all-purpose flour into the milk-yogurt mixture. Cover, and leave in a warm place to proof for 3 to 5 days.

7. At the end of 5 days, your starter should be bubbly and about the consistency of pancake batter. When it has reached this point, place the jar in the refrigerator for storage.

Sourdough French Bread

An old favorite, this bread has a long history. Its simple ingredients made it a favorite of the forty-niners and a San Francisco staple.

1½-pound	*1-pound*
1½ teaspoons active dry yeast	1 teaspoon active dry yeast
1 teaspoon sugar	1 teaspoon sugar
3 cups bread flour	2 cups bread flour
1 teaspoon salt	1 teaspoon salt
½ cup sourdough starter	¼ cup sourdough starter
¾ cup warm water	½ cup warm water

Notes
1. For Panasonic/National machines, use 2½ teaspoons of yeast for the 1½-pound loaf.
2. If your machine has a "French bread" setting, use that setting for this recipe.

Nutritional Analysis

	1½-pound	*1-pound*	
Total calories	1758	1136	calories
Total protein	59	38	grams
Total carbohydrates	353	228	grams
Total fat	8	5	grams
Total saturated fat	1	1	grams
Total cholesterol	0	0	milligrams
Total sodium	2141	2138	milligrams
Total fibre	8	5	grams
Calories from fat	4	4	percent

Sourdough Rye Bread

This sourdough-and-rye combination is excellent for morning toast or for ham-and-cheese sandwiches. It has the flavor and texture of rye bread and a distinct sourdough aroma and taste.

1½-pound	1-pound
2 teaspoons active dry yeast	1½ teaspoons active dry yeast
2½ cups bread flour	1½ cups bread flour
1½ tablespoons unsweetened cocoa	1 tablespoon unsweetened cocoa
1 teaspoon salt	½ teaspoon salt
2 teaspoons dill weed	1½ teaspoons dill weed
1½ teaspoons caraway seed	1 teaspoon caraway seed
¾ cup rye flour	½ cup rye flour
1 tablespoon butter	2 teaspoons butter
1 egg	1 egg
2 teaspoons molasses	½ tablespoon molasses
1 tablespoon olive oil	½ tablespoon olive oil
3 ounces warm water	¼ cup warm water
¾ cup sourdough starter	½ cup sourdough starter

Note: For Panasonic/National machines, use 3 teaspoons of yeast for the 1½-pound loaf.

Nutritional Analysis

	1½-pound	1-pound	
Total calories	2275	1473	calories
Total protein	74	52	grams
Total carbohydrates	401	256	grams
Total fat	41	27	grams
Total saturated fat	12	8	grams
Total cholesterol	244	234	milligrams
Total sodium	2241	1148	milligrams
Total fibre	9	6	grams
Calories from fat	16	16	percent

Sourdough Onion Rye Bread

If you are looking for a tangy bread, look no further. This bread combines the tart flavor of sourdough with the distinct taste of onion, rye, and caraway seed. The result is a flavorful bread that is great for sandwiches. This was a favorite of the rye-bread tasters.

1½-pound	1-pound
1½ teaspoons active dry yeast	1 teaspoon active dry yeast
1½ tablespoons gluten (optional)	1 tablespoon gluten (optional)
1 teaspoon caraway seeds	½ teaspoon caraway seeds
1½ cups bread flour	¾ cup bread flour
3 tablespoons onion-soup mix	2 tablespoons onion-soup mix
1 cup rye flour	¾ cup rye flour
½ cup whole-wheat flour	¼ cup whole-wheat flour
½ cup sourdough starter	¼ cup sourdough starter
2 tablespoons warm milk	1½ tablespoons warm milk
1 tablespoon olive oil	2 teaspoons olive oil
1 tablespoon vinegar	2 teaspoons vinegar
2 teaspoons molasses	1 teaspoon molasses
7 ounces warm water	4½ ounces warm water

Note: For Panasonic/National machines, use 3 teaspoons of yeast for the 1½-pound loaf.

Nutritional Analysis

	1½-pound	1-pound	
Total calories	1919	1137	calories
Total protein	72	46	grams
Total carbohydrates	364	212	grams
Total fat	24	16	grams
Total saturated fat	3	2	grams
Total cholesterol	1	1	milligrams
Total sodium	2898	1918	milligrams
Total fibre	15	8	grams
Calories from fat	11	13	percent

Sourdough Whole-Wheat Bread

Sourdough lovers will enjoy this variation of ordinary whole-wheat bread. This is a simple, low-calorie, low-fat bread that is nutritious as well as delicious.

1½-pound	*1-pound*
1½ teaspoons active dry yeast	1 teaspoon active dry yeast
1 tablespoon gluten (optional)	2 teaspoons gluten (optional)
1 tablespoon dough enhancer (optional)	2 teaspoons dough enhancer (optional)
½ cup bread flour	½ cup bread flour
2½ cups whole-wheat flour	1½ cups whole-wheat flour
1 teaspoon salt	1 teaspoon salt
1½ teaspoons olive oil	1 teaspoon olive oil
1 cup warm water	5½ ounces warm water
½ cup sourdough starter	¼ cup sourdough starter

Note: For Panasonic/National machines, use 2½ teaspoons of yeast for the 1½-pound loaf.

Nutritional Analysis

	1½-pound	*1-pound*	
Total calories	1559	1152	calories
Total protein	58	42	grams
Total carbohydrates	318	231	grams
Total fat	12	10	grams
Total saturated fat	2	2	grams
Total cholesterol	0	0	milligrams
Total sodium	2138	2137	milligrams
Total fibre	40	25	grams
Calories from fat	7	8	percent

Sourdough Sesame Bread

This is a combination of sourdough and whole wheat, enhanced with the nutty flavor of sesame seeds. Serve it warm with any soup or salad.

1½-pound	1-pound
1½ teaspoons active dry yeast	1 teaspoon active dry yeast
½ cup sesame seeds	5 tablespoons sesame seeds
1 cup whole-wheat flour	¾ cup whole-wheat flour
1½ cups bread flour	1 cup bread flour
1 teaspoon salt	½ teaspoon salt
1 egg	1 egg
2 tablespoons lemon juice	4 teaspoons lemon juice
2 tablespoons honey	4 teaspoons honey
5 ounces warm water	3½ ounces warm water
½ cup sourdough starter	¼ cup sourdough starter

Notes
1. For Panasonic/National machines, use 3 teaspoons of yeast for the 1½-pound loaf.
2. For DAK/Welbilt machines, use ¾ cup of warm water for the 1½-pound loaf.

Nutritional Analysis

	1½-pound	1-pound	
Total calories	2019	1346	calories
Total protein	70	48	grams
Total carbohydrates	337	223	grams
Total fat	48	32	grams
Total saturated fat	7	5	grams
Total cholesterol	213	213	milligrams
Total sodium	2210	1139	milligrams
Total fibre	23	16	grams
Calories from fat	21	21	percent

Sourdough Dill Bread

Here, you'll find the classic taste of dill bread with a trace of sourdough aroma. This is a splendid variation of dill bread that is excellent for sandwiches, particularly tuna salad.

1½-pound	1-pound
1½ teaspoons active dry yeast	1 teaspoon active dry yeast
2 tablespoons sugar	1½ tablespoons sugar
3 cups bread flour	2 cups bread flour
1 teaspoon salt	½ teaspoon salt
2 tablespoons dill weed	4 teaspoons dill weed
1 egg	1 egg
¾ cup cottage cheese	½ cup cottage cheese
3 ounces warm water	¼ cup warm water
½ cup sourdough starter	¼ cup sourdough starter

Note: For Panasonic/National machines, use 2½ teaspoons of yeast for the 1½-pound loaf.

Nutritional Analysis

	1½-pound	1-pound	
Total calories	2078	1377	calories
Total protein	87	59	grams
Total carbohydrates	383	249	grams
Total fat	16	12	grams
Total saturated fat	4	3	grams
Total cholesterol	236	228	milligrams
Total sodium	2981	1653	milligrams
Total fibre	8	5	grams
Calories from fat	7	8	percent

BREAD DOUGHS
YOU FINISH YOURSELF

If you get tired of making the same-shaped breads and are willing to do a little bit of the work, you can use your machine to make the dough and then you can take it from there. Actually, any recipe in this book can be finished by hand, but this section primarily contains recipes that, because of their shape, can't be finished in the bread machine. Two of the recipes, French Bread and Bohemian Rye, could be finished in the machine, but are more authentic in their traditional shapes.

French Bread

A traditional French bread recipe, this is easy to make and yields a beautiful and tasty loaf.

1½-pound	*1-pound*
2½ teaspoons active dry yeast	1½ teaspoons active dry yeast
3 cups bread flour	2 cups bread flour
1½ teaspoons salt	1 teaspoon salt
1 cup warm water	5½ ounces warm water

Note: For Panasonic/National machines, use 3 teaspoons of yeast for the 1½-pound loaf.

Instructions for baking: Remove from the machine after the first rise is complete (or use the dough cycle if your machine has one). After removal from the machine, knead the dough for 5–10 minutes. Shape the dough into a large loaf; then place the dough on a baking pan or sheet that has been liberally sprinkled with cornmeal. Cover with a cloth and let the dough rise for 30–40 minutes.

After the bread has risen, use a sharp knife or razor blade to make diagonal cuts on the top of the loaf. Bake the loaf at 410 degrees for 30–40 minutes.

If a hard crust is desired, place a pan of water in the oven with the bread while it is baking. For a soft crust, cover the outside of the loaf with a water-and-egg-white mixture before baking.

To enhance the flavor and appearance, apply a fine spray of water before baking and then sprinkle the bread with a coating of sesame seeds.

Nutritional Analysis

	1½-pound	*1-pound*	
Total calories	1503	1001	calories
Total protein	52	34	grams
Total carbohydrates	300	200	grams
Total fat	7	5	grams
Total saturated fat	1	1	grams
Total cholesterol	0	0	milligrams
Total sodium	3207	2138	milligrams
Total fibre	7	5	grams
Calories from fat	4	4	percent

Pizza Dough

A high-rising pizza dough that makes one large pizza (using the 1½-pound recipe) or one medium pizza (using the 1-pound recipe). It is simple to make and lets you create your own pizzas, using the toppings you like.

1½-pound

3 teaspoons active dry yeast

2 tablespoons sugar

3 cups all-purpose flour

1 teaspoon salt

2 teaspoons olive oil

1 cup warm water

1-pound

2 teaspoons active dry yeast

1½ tablespoons sugar

2 cups all-purpose flour

1 teaspoon salt

1½ teaspoons olive oil

5½ ounces warm water

Note: Use the dough cycle, if your machine has one, or remove the dough from the bread machine after the first rise has been completed.

Instructions for baking: After removing the pizza dough from the bread machine, punch the dough down. Then place it in a greased bowl, cover it with a cloth, and let it rise in a warm place for 30–40 minutes.

Remove the dough from the bowl and roll it out flat. Place the dough on a pizza pan that has been sprinkled with cornmeal, and finish stretching the dough until it is a uniform thickness throughout. Spread tomato sauce on the pizza and finish with toppings of your choice. Bake the pizza at 350 degrees for 10–15 minutes or until the crust turns light brown.

Nutritional Analysis
(Not Including Pizza Toppings)

	1½-pound	1-pound	
Total calories	1585	1064	calories
Total protein	52	35	grams
Total carbohydrates	301	201	grams
Total fat	16	12	grams
Total saturated fat	2	2	grams
Total cholesterol	0	0	milligrams
Total sodium	2142	2139	milligrams
Total fibre	7	5	grams
Calories from fat	9	10	percent

Breadsticks

Instead of sliced bread, try serving breadsticks with your spaghetti or lasagna dinner. These are easy and fun to make.

1½-pound	1-pound
1½ teaspoons active dry yeast	1 teaspoon active dry yeast
3 cups bread flour	2 cups bread flour
1½ teaspoons salt	1 teaspoon salt
1 cup warm water	5 ounces warm water
2 tablespoons olive oil	4 teaspoons olive oil

Notes
1. For Panasonic/National machines, use 3 teaspoons of yeast for the 1½-pound loaf.
2. For DAK/Welbilt machines, use an extra 2 tablespoons of water with the 1½-pound recipe.
3. Use the dough cycle, if your machine has one, or remove the dough from the bread machine after the first rise is completed.
4. Try substituting garlic salt for regular salt for a garlic-bread taste.
5. Add 3 tablespoons of onion soup mix for onion-flavored breadsticks.

Instructions for baking: Remove the dough from the machine and knead it for approximately 5–6 minutes, punching the dough to remove all the air. Form the dough into sticks by pinching balls of dough and rolling them with your hands into cylinder-shaped pieces. Lay the sticks in a pan that has been dusted with cornmeal. Place the sticks about 1 inch from each other in the pan.

Let the breadsticks rise for approximately 45 minutes or until almost doubled in size. Bake them in a 375-degree oven for 15–20 minutes or until golden brown. For a crunchy crust, place a pan of water in the oven with the breadsticks while baking. If desired, brush a water-and-egg-white mixture on the breadsticks before baking and coat with sesame seeds.

Nutritional Analysis

	1½-pound	1-pound	
Total calories	1734	1156	calories
Total protein	51	34	grams
Total carbohydrates	300	200	grams
Total fat	34	23	grams

Total saturated fat	5	3	grams
Total cholesterol	0	0	milligrams
Total sodium	3206	2137	milligrams
Total fibre	7	4	grams
Calories from fat	18	18	percent

Bagels

These are traditional water bagels with a dense texture and great flavor. They are great in the morning with cream cheese or butter.

1½-pound

2½ teaspoons active dry yeast

3 cups all-purpose flour

1½ teaspoons salt

1½ tablespoons sugar

9 ounces warm water

1-pound

1½ teaspoons active dry yeast

2 cups all-purpose flour

1 teaspoon salt

1 tablespoon sugar

¾ cup warm water

Notes
1. For Panasonic/National machines, use 3 teaspoons of yeast for the 1½-pound recipe.
2. For DAK/Welbilt machines, use 10 ounces of warm water for the 1½-pound recipe.
3. If your machine has one, use the dough cycle. If it does not, remove the dough at the end of the first rise.
4. For onion bagels, add 3 tablespoons of onion-soup mix.
5. For garlic bagels, use garlic salt instead of regular salt.

Instructions for baking: Remove the dough from the bread machine. Punch it down and knead it for 5–6 minutes. Form the dough into small (2 inches in diameter) balls. Flatten the balls slightly and use your thumb or finger to punch a hole into the middle of each bagel. Place the bagels on a lightly floured baking sheet, cover them with a cloth, and let them rise for approximately 30 minutes.

In the meantime, prepare a water-and-sugar mixture consisting of 6 cups of water and ½ tablespoon of sugar. Bring this mixture to a boil in a pan and adjust the heat to maintain a steady boil. Boil each bagel for approximately 5 minutes in the solution, turning frequently. Then place the bagels on a baking sheet coated with cornmeal. Brush the bagels with egg (whole eggs whipped) and bake in a 400-degree oven for 20–25 minutes or until brown.

Nutritional Analysis

	1½-pound	1-pound	
Total calories	1572	1047	calories
Total protein	52	34	grams
Total carbohydrates	318	212	grams
Total fat	7	5	grams
Total saturated fat	1	1	grams
Total cholesterol	0	0	milligrams
Total sodium	3207	2138	milligrams
Total fibre	7	5	grams
Calories from fat	4	4	percent

Bohemian Rye Bread

This bread is made with 100-percent rye flour. Since rye flour doesn't rise much, it is best to bake this loaf in the traditional round shape. Rye lovers will enjoy the pure rye flavor and authentic Bohemian taste of this loaf.

1½-pound	1-pound
2 teaspoons active dry yeast	1½ teaspoons active dry yeast
3 tablespoons gluten	2 tablespoons gluten
2 teaspoons sugar	1½ teaspoons sugar
2 teaspoons caraway seed	1½ teaspoons caraway seed
3 cups rye flour	2 cups rye flour
2 teaspoons salt	1½ teaspoons salt
5 ounces warm water	½ cup warm water
½ cup sour cream	¼ cup sour cream

Notes
1. For Panasonic/National machines, use 3 teaspoons of yeast for the 1½-pound loaf.

2. For DAK/Welbilt machines, use 6 ounces of warm water for the 1½-pound loaf.
3. Use the dough cycle, if your machine has one, or remove the dough after the first rise is complete.

Instructions for baking: Remove the dough from the bread machine. Punch it down and knead it for approximately 5–6 minutes. Place the kneaded dough in a greased bowl and cover it with a cloth. Let it rise in a warm location for approximately 60 minutes.

Remove the dough from the bowl and shape it into a round or oblong loaf. Place the loaf on a baking sheet that has been liberally sprinkled with cornmeal. Cut two or three slits in the top of the loaf with a sharp knife or razor blade. Bake in a 375-degree oven for 30–35 minutes.

Nutritional Analysis

	1½-pound	1-pound	
Total calories	1700	1097	calories
Total protein	83	55	grams
Total carbohydrates	294	196	grams
Total fat	37	20	grams
Total saturated fat	16	8	grams
Total cholesterol	51	26	milligrams
Total sodium	4336	3236	milligrams
Total fibre	9	6	grams
Calories from fat	19	17	percent

Pan Dulce

Pan Dulce is Mexican sweet bread. Because of its sweet flavor and light texture, it is a traditional partner to a cup of Mexican hot chocolate.

1½-pound	1-pound
2 teaspoons active dry yeast	1½ teaspoons active dry yeast
3½ cups all-purpose flour	2 cups all-purpose flour
¼ cup sugar	2½ tablespoons sugar
½ teaspoon salt	½ teaspoon salt
2 eggs	1 egg

3½ tablespoons butter	2½ tablespoons butter
1 cup warm milk	5½ ounces warm milk

Notes
1. For Panasonic/National machines, use 3 teaspoons of yeast for the 1½-pound size.
2. Use the dough cycle, if your machine has one, or remove the dough after the first rise.

Instructions for baking: While the bread is rising in your machine, prepare a streusel by mixing ¾ cup of sugar with ¾ cup of all-purpose flour. Add 4 tablespoons of butter and 2 egg yolks. Mix together until well blended. If you don't wish to make your pan dulces with streusel, you can make up a simple cinnamon-sugar combination instead by blending ½ cup of sugar with 4 tablespoons of cinnamon.

After removing the dough from the machine, punch down the dough and separate into small (about 2 inches in diameter) balls of dough. Roll each ball flat with a rolling pin on a floured surface. Spread the streusel or cinnamon-sugar mixture onto the rolled-out dough ball, and then roll up the dough, similar to a cinnamon roll. Place on a cookie sheet about 2 inches apart and let rise for 30–60 minutes or until doubled in size.

After the rolls have about doubled in size, make slits in the top with a sharp knife or razor blade and bake in a 375-degree oven for 15–18 minutes or until the top of the rolls are light brown.

Nutritional Analysis (Not Including Streusel)

	1½-pound	1-pound	
Total calories	2533	1511	calories
Total protein	80	46	grams
Total carbohydrates	410	239	grams
Total fat	61	40	grams
Total saturated fat	31	21	grams
Total cholesterol	545	297	milligrams
Total sodium	1328	1222	milligrams
Total fibre	8	5	grams
Calories from fat	22	24	percent

APPENDIX

Measures

Table 4: Dry Measure Equivalencies

To ➡️ From	teaspoon	tablespoon	cup	pint
teaspoon	1	3	48	96
tablespoon	1/3	1	16	32
cup	1/48	1/16	1	2
pint	1/96	1/48	1/2	1

Table 5: Liquid Measure Equivalencies

To ➡️ From	teaspoon	tablespoon	ounce	cup	pint
teaspoon	1	3	6	48	96
tablespoon	1/3	1	2	16	32
ounce	1/6	1/2	1	8	16
cup	1/48	1/16	1/8	1	2
pint	1/96	1/48	1/16	1/2	1

Nutritional Quick Reference

All of the recipes in this book were analyzed for nutritional value. The following are lists containing the top 10 breads in each category, in order.

Highest-Fibre Breads

Seven-Grain Bread
100% Wheat Bread
Dill Wheat Bread
Whole-Wheat Bagel Bread
Corn Rye Bread
Whole-Wheat Oat Cinnamon Raisin Bread
Sourdough Whole-Wheat Bread
Whole-Wheat Three-Seed Bread
Russian Black Bread
Carrot-Celery Bread

Lowest-Fat-Content Breads

Whole-Wheat Bagel Bread
French Bread (dough)
Bagels (dough)
Sourdough French Bread
Onion French Bread
100% Wheat Bread
Sourdough Whole-Wheat Bread
Sourdough Dill Bread
Pizza (dough)
Swedish Limpa Rye Bread

Lowest-Calorie Breads

Whole-Wheat Bagel Bread
French Bread (dough)
Corn Rye Bread
Sourdough Whole-Wheat Bread
Bagels (dough)
Zucchini Bread
Pizza (dough)
Carrot-Celery Bread
Onion French Bread
Oat-Bran Bread

Lowest-Sodium Breads

Yorkshire Spice Bread
Peppy Cheese Bread
Apple Bread
Corn Rye Bread
Orange Bread
Cranberry Bread
Apple-Butter Bread
Carrot Bread
Cracked-Wheat Bread
Banana Oat-Bran Bread

Overall Healthiest Breads

A formula was used to find the best 10 breads, based on their combination of low-calories, low-sodium, low-fat, and high-fibre content.
Corn Rye Bread
Sourdough Whole-Wheat Bread
Whole-Wheat Oat Cinnamon Raisin Bread
100% Wheat Bread
Whole-Wheat Bagel Bread
Seven-Grain Bread
Carrot-Celery Bread
Apple Bread
Banana Oat-Bran Bread
Dill Wheat Bread

Bread Machine Information

Use this space to enter specific information about your bread machine and then use it as a handy reference.

Machine Brand _____

Model Number _____

Capacity (1 or 1½ pounds) _____

Basic White-Bread Recipe:

Bread Flour _____

Ounces of Liquid _____

Liquidity Ratio _____

INDEX